Islam,
Christianity,
and
African Identity

Islam, Christianity, and African Identity

Sulayman S. Nyang

AMANA BOOKS
58 Elliot Street
Brattleboro, Vermont 05301

Designed by Chris Nerlinger
Printed in the United States of America

Islam, Christianity, and African Identity

Sulayman S. Nyang

AMANA BOOKS
58 Elliot Street
Brattleboro, Vermont 05301

Designed by Chris Nerlinger
Printed in the United States of America

ACKNOWLEDGEMENT

We are grateful to the following publishers for permission to reproduce some of my articles which appeared in their publications: 1. Howard University's *New Direction* for my paper on "Traditional African Thought" published in October, 1980; 2. *Islamiyyat*, the journal of Kebangsaan University in Malaysia for my paper on "Islam and the African World," published on Volune 3, 1981; 3. *UNESCO Courier* for my paper on "The World of Islam. The Impact on Black Africa," published in August/September, 1981, and for my paper on "An African Cosmology," published in February, 1982.

TABLE OF CONTENTS

INTRODUCTION

*A*t this point in the history of African man the question of identity and self-definition seems to occupy a prominent place in his world of ideas. Indeed, many attempts at self-definition have already been made, and though none has actually seized full control of the mental worlds of all Africans, or most of Africa's children at home and abroad, the intellectual building blocks that went into the architectural design and construction of these different intellectual temples now beckoning for converts are, by all reckoning, diverse and eclectic.[1] This dominant characteristic of present African intellectual life is a vivid manifestation of the African historical experience. African man, it should be remembered, has spent over the last million years battling against the calamities and hazards of nature on the one hand, and the military and cultural imperialisms of human invaders hailing from different geographical points outside his continent, on the other.

This paper is a philosophical and historical analysis of African responses to the civilizational challenges coming from Europe and Arabia. Rather than focus primarily on the African's mental and spiritual encounters with nature, and the resulting belief system that came to dominate his intellectual and mental horizons, this study wishes to examine the African encounters with the Abrahamic tradition and the balance sheet that can be drawn since the first encounter.

All these encounters with foreign invaders exposed Africa and her peoples to new ideas and new tyrannies. Such misfortunes and calamities often created a crisis of identity and a sense of alienation among those peoples of the continent who were forced by circumstances to live under alien rule. Not all foreign intrusions into Africa, however, led to identity crisis and alienation. There were instances in the early history of the continent when many African peoples lived peacefully and comfortably with their foreigners. This was true in ancient Egypt when the Assyrians, Greeks, and Romans, respectively, conquered the African inhabitants of the Nile Valley and used their power and influence to spread their culture to the major centers of civilization in conquered Egypt. The Arab invaders of the Maghrib were, of course, fiercely resisted by the Berber indigenes of the continent, but as the dust settled and more and more intermarriages took place between the Arabs and the Berbers, the Arab language and culture gained ground in Berberland.

In making references to these major landmarks in African history, we should also bear in mind that in all these previous encounters between the inhabitants of the continent and the outsiders from the northern Mediterranean and the Arabian Peninsula, not all the peoples of the continent underwent simultaneously the agony of military defeat or the shock of foreign cultural penetration. This came about only with the European exploration of the interior of the continent and the subsequent conquest and colonization of the entire land mass called Africa. Indeed, if one can speak of a genuine African identity as such, one must trace it to European colonialism. It was actually the European man, whose emotional involvement with nationalism made it imperative for him to search for something that could convince him of his own identity and existence, who introduced into the African consciousness the notion of a nation/state. Having witnessed the gradual collapse of the supporting pillars of a unified Christendom, and after having gone through a very bloody experience in religious warfare among the numerous sects in post-Reformation Europe, secularistic thinkers among the peoples of that continent began to build new ideological bridges which, they thought, their alienated fellows could use to cross the swelling rivers of spiritual uncertainty.

Nationalism and racism, two ideologies that affected the consciousness of Western man in the nineteenth and twentieth centuries, provided the necessary tools to change the world in the new image of Europe. The outcome for Africa of this European attempt at self-definition, in an age of galloping secularism, was cultural and racial alienation. The atrocities committed against Africans in the name of Western civilization created a deep wound in the African psyche. Such a phenomenon imposed upon the different peoples of the continent a new name and a new image in the eyes of all Europeans. This phenomenon, whose nature and peculiarities have been dissected and analyzed very well by Frantz Fanon, came to be called the *colonial mentality* or *colonial alienation.*[2]

Writing on this African encounter, but from a Christian viewpoint, Father Mveng of Cameroon has argued that the early stages of missionary activities in the continent were not very positive because the church was, at the beginning, not living up to the message of Christ. Rather than deal with the African personality and encourage a dialogue between such a personality and the Church of Christ, many of these early missionaries wanted to destroy the African personality before embarking upon the teaching of the Christian message. Such wanton acts, Father Mveng maintains, led to *depersonalization*. This phenomenon was a result of the mode of teaching developed by the missionaries. As the African father puts it:

> ...the schools remained a medium for missionary apologetics. They were a way of transmitting religious instruction. They were a medium for spreading values which ignored the traditional patrimony of culture. And indeed, these values were often in a state of war against this patrimony. So in their turn the schools provoked the crisis of identity...[3]

This crisis of identity was one day to show itself to be the crisis of depersonalization. Father Mveng believes that the African encounter with the West has resulted in a serious crisis which has serious implications for African man and his future. He argues, and quite cogently, that the depersonalization of the African has led to his poverty on many levels: material, sociological, emotional, cultural and religious. What the Father is saying is that the collapse of traditional African culture during the period of colonialism has made the life of the African empty and confused. No longer at ease in the world he traditionally lived in, deprived of the social and psychological tools which make life safe, comfortable and controllable, and condemned to lead a life of cultural poverty and dependence, the alienated African becomes the proverbial donkey who must gallop faster and faster in order to grasp the western cultural carrot dangled before his eyes. Such a life of cultural mimicry and lack of originality exposes the African man to deep psychological and psycho-cultural problems. The only way out of this crisis is a willingness to go back to the traditional sources. This, in the African father's view, is the only way the Church of Christ can maintain a dialogue with Africa; for such a dialogue means that "Africa agrees to become Christian insofar as Christianity agrees to become African."[4]

The last point, which I think was well put by Father Mveng, is his contention that alienation as known in Europe is different from alienation in Africa. He compares the crisis of identity in Africa today to what the fall of Rome in 430 A.D. meant to the Roman contemporaries of St. Augustine. In fact, he argues that "the situation in Africa is far more critical than the fall of Rome in 430."[5] In his belief, the categories of alienation are inadequate to describe the experiences of the African peoples, who were subjected to almost every form of humiliation and exploitation. The children of Africa have been enslaved for centuries and sold by auction in markets around the world. They were colonized and made victims of a systematic destruction of cultural identity and personality. All these woes and wounds suffered by the children of Africa combined to make the African crisis one of *annihilation* rather than alienation.

It is evident from the foregoing discussion that what is generally referred to as the African identity is the common heritage of colonial exploitation and racial discrimination which the peoples of the African continent suffered at the hands of slavers and colonial rulers. An American writer, Victor C. Ferkiss, echoing the views of many other observers of the African scene, writes:

> The unity of Africa was forged by the common experience of European domination and the common venture of overthrowing that domination. Africa is a creation not of common race or geography or culture but of a common experience in world politics. ...It was not economic or political domination per se that was the essence of colonial rule, but racial subordination. It is this which has determined the essence of African self-identity — not a common genetic heritage but a common reaction to a racial attitude on the part of colonial rulers.[6]

This interpretation of the African experience has now become the dominant understanding of what African nationalism or Pan-Africanism means. In other words, the African identity is generally defined negatively, and this is largely due to the fact that it is assumed to be the psychological and psychohistorical adhesive which unites the variegated members of the colonially created community of African suffering. This point was not lost to men like Nkrumah of Ghana. To him Africa is a geographic as well as a historical entity, and for this and other reasons, he refused to accept the colonial idea that Africa was an extension of Europe.

Writing on the concept of "We are all Africans," Ali A. Mazrui gives a very incisive analysis of the question of African identity. His analysis does not only show the men like Nkrumah and Nyerere accepted in their pronouncements views like the one stated above by Ferkiss, but that their nationalism is different from Euopean nationalism in the sense that, in the African experience, these African nationalists fought foreign racial rulers who were themselves not natives of the African continent. In Mazrui's view, this assertion of the African identity makes African nationalism "more egalitarian than libertarian in its aspirations." This is so because, to the African nationalists, independence means racial equality is also related to the position of African dignity. Hence, Mazrui's argument that African nationalism is "dignitarian."[7] Yet, such psycho-analytic explanation, Thomas Hodgkin tells us, betrays a "residual intellectual colonialism" which only serves "to strengthen the common, but mistaken, Western view that Africa is a special case, its revolution unlike other revolutions in human history."[8]

Regardless of whether one is of the "dignitarian" persuasion (to borrow James S. Coleman's phraseology) or not, the fact still remains that the twentieth century presents an African continent whose peoples have rallied around the banner of political independence from alien rule. The sense of unity demonstrated throughout the struggle against the forces of imperialism and colonialism made it abundantly clear that the variegated ethnic elements of the colonial territories were willing to sink their differences, at least temporarily, and fight arduously for the liberation of their lands. In my view, the anti-colonial struggle in Africa was the political manifestation of a Panethnic African attitude towards all foreign rulers.

Even though it may be true, as Jamal M. Ahmad argues in a brilliantly constructed essay,[9] that the fluidity of the African scene makes it very difficult in the 1960's for one to talk of Africanness or African aspirations, one can still argue that, when seen from the wider perspective of history, the African revolution of the late fifties and early sixties might well be the permanent concretization of what started out as a colonial idea. Again, it should be stated that the Western colonialist imposed a common label on the diverse peoples of the continent, and this imported identity was accepted by the nationalists who felt that the best way to fight the European colonial masters was to turn their ideological tables against them. One of these tables was the term and concept Africa. Henceforth, the word African was to become politically explosive, and its psychological and psychohistorical meanings for the African were to be far from what the colonialists had dreamed earlier.

Yet, in noting this sense of unity created by the colonial presence, we must also point out that not all Africans agree on the meaning and content of Africanity. There are, as far as I can see it, three concentric circles of African identities. Each African is forced by a concatenation of circumstances to reconcile the three competing loyalties locked in

soul. If he is, for example, a Wolof from the Senegambia, he must live
with his blackness, a community of biological fate which he shares with
all those who see themselves as blacks and are accepted as such by
racially significant others. While facing up to the challenges of the
racial divide, he must also confront the demands made upon him by the
state system which he and the other politically conscious inhabitants of
Gambia and Senegal inherited from the recently departed colonial
masters. Last but not least, he must also patiently and prudently carry
upon his head the psychological and psycho-historical baggage which
his bloodline and culture have unloaded on him since his initiation as a
member of his ethnic community.[10]

These three competing loyalties, which, by the way, are not necessarily mutually exclusive all the time, affect the thinking of many Africans.
In fact, I am inclined to believe that within the African continent there
are two dominant positions regarding the question, who is an African?

First, there are the continental Pan-Africanists who believe in the
unity and sanctity of the geographical entity called Africa. These
advocates of Pan-Africanism strongly believe that the term African can
be legitimately applied to anyone who makes Africa his or her home,
takes part in African history, proudly labors for her political and
economic development, and modestly and devotedly follow the princi-
ples of majority rule in the governmental processes of African societies.

This first position was embraced by the late Kwame Nkrumah. He
spelled out his views on this subject early in his political career. During
a very successful visit to the state of Liberia, the former Ghanaian leader
addressed himself to the racial question and to the African identity
problem in the following manner:

> I do not believe in racialism or tribalism. The concept "Africa for the
> Africans" does not mean that other races are excluded from it. No, it
> only means that Africans can and must govern themselves in their own
> countries without imperialist or foreign impositions, but that peoples of
> other races can remain on African soil, carry on their legitimate avoca-
> tions, live on terms of peace, friendship and equality with Africans on
> their own soil.....*[11]

The above statement is one of many which amply demonstrate the
Nkrumahist commitment to a continental vision of Africa. Nkrumah, as
most commentators would agree, was never convinced by the colonial
notion of an African continent divided by a vast Sahara Desert. In fact,

the Ghanaian leader wasted no time to prove that he was a man wedded to the continental vision and he symbolically demonstrated his ideological sincerity by contracting a marriage with an African lady from the land of the Pharaohs.

Besides the continental Pan-Africanists, there are the Sub-Saharan Pan-Africanists whose version is that of a united black humanity in Africa. Rather than embrace the Arabo-Berber populations north of the Sahara Desert, these advocates of residential Pan-Negroism define them out of the equation and decree that such non-black elements who reside on the continent can be accepted as members of the African community only when they sever all ties with their allies or kith and kin in Europe and/or Arabia. Obafemi Awolowo of Nigeria has generally been identified with this position.[12]

Given these differences of opinion regarding the African identity, this writer finds it necessary to take account of both interpretations in the subsequent pages. Thus, when talking about the Islamic invasion, for example, I will see it as an assault on Berber and Sub-Saharan African cultural zones by the Arab standard-bearers of Islam. In doing so, I will be looking at the encounter from the perspective of the continental Pan-Africanists who believe in the geographical unity and sanctity of the continent.

Again, when the colonial experience is examined, the level of analysis will shift, depending upon the issues discussed and the time covered. However, it should be pointed out that, because of the nature and manifestations of colonialism in Sub-Saharan Africa, this study will focus largely on the dialectical relationship between the Black inhabitants of the continent and the Euro-Western colonizers of the 19th century. This is due, to a large extent, to the peculiarities associated with the arrival of European colonial power in Africa. As Father Mveng correctly pointed out, the African, and most specifically the African Christian, must grapple with the problem of annihilation.

This study, which is an exploratory and not a very exhaustive one, deals with two Abrahamic religions and their individual and collective challenges to African man. By Abrahamic religion I mean the three Semitic religions of Judaism, Christianity, and Islam. The last two religions are selected for discussion because, since the beginning of recorded history, they alone have invaded and dominated considerably the African's physical and mental worlds, and the results of such encroachments have driven many a traditional African to psycho-cultural confusion, if not to soul-searching redefinition of self and community.

This book studies three major aspects of the relationship between two Abrahamic religions and African civilization. First of all, it describes the traditional African cosmological understanding of man, his nature and destiny in the cosmos. Secondly, it examines the intrusion of Islam into the African's consciousness; and with regard to this particular aspect of the study, the author also intends to demonstrate in the subsequent pages how, to some extent, the religion of Islam has taught the African man to adopt a conception of self and of reality which is alien to his original vision of life and reality. Furthermore, this work, in pursuit of its analytical objectives, also examines the impact of Islam on the psychological, psycho-cultural and psycho-historical activities of African man.

In the third chapter of this study, a serious analysis of western colonialism and its impact on African religious life is undertaken. It is argued that the colonial association with Christianity gravely affected its image in Africa. Yet, in noting this aspect of the African encounter with Euro-Western Christianity, I should hasten to add that the Christian missionaries did make significant contributions to the material and intellectual development of Africa. This is equally true of both branches of the Abrahamic tree of religion.

In the fourth chapter, two major African thinkers are selected for study and analysis. The writings of the late Kwame Nkrumah of Ghana and President Leopold Senghor of Senegal are examined with the intention of identifying the solutions they offer to the African identity problem. As we will see later, to Kwame Nkrumah the African identity problem stems from the colonial experience. He believes that the post-colonial era is a very trying period for the African, because he is confronted with three competing ideologies which must be reconciled within a socialist framework if the African personality is to be felt in world history. The three strands of thought to which Nkrumah refers are the traditional values of Old Africa, the Islamic heritage of a large portion of Africa's population, and the Euro-Western Christian legacy of the colonial period. Besides the writings of Nkrumah, the author also examines the works of Senghor with the intention of identifying his prescriptions for the New Africa. As a leader in the Negritude Movement, Senghor believes that the African personality is different from the European personality in the sense that his attitude towards life and the world is the opposite of the rationalistic, antagonistic and discursive attitude of the European mind.

In the final chapter, I offer my conclusions to the reader. In my view, the African encounter with the Abrahamic tradition has been very inspiring and spiritually elevating. The message of Abraham, as echoed and preached by the Old Testament prophets, Christ and Muhammad, is still reverberating in the African spiritual firmaments. The ringing of church bells and the booming voices of latter-day Bilals summoning fellow believers to prayer, make it crystal clear to all observers that Africa has finally joined the growing commonwealth of believers in the Abrahamic tradition. The African decision to embrace the Abrahamic tradition is significant in many respects. One could make the argument that the African peoples have fulfilled, in some ways, the three most important messages of the Abrahamic religions. We can assert with Edward Blyden that the Black man is the only sentient and rational human creature who has served all *humanity*. Just as Christ, in Christian theology, is said to have died for humanity after having taken the form of human flesh, so we can say without any blasphemy that the African has suffered more the humiliations and psychological defeats associated with the *cross of color* than any other human being. Again, we can also maintain, that just as the children of Israel have labored and toiled as the slaves of Pharaoanic Egypt, so can we too say that Africa's children have groaned under the thick boots of an enslaving majority in the Americas. Last but not least, we can also say that some form of ecological Jihad was waged by Africa's children not only against human invaders who have tried to impose the tyranny of self-deified men, which in my view is the highest form of idolatry, but have struggled with great dignity to humanize the African ecosystem under very unfavorable natural odds.

To put it another way, I would say that the African encounter with the Abrahamic tradition is going to be, in the long run, beneficial to the Africans as well as their fellow worshippers elsewhere on the planet. Africa's gift to the followers of the Abrahamic tradition will be the spirit of cultural tolerance in a world of ethnic diversity. One thing that should serve as food for global thought is the African capability to co-exist with so many hundreds of neighboring cultural systems within a very limited space. In a world that is shrinking very fast as a result of the technological revolution, and again in a world where the knowledge explosion is giving rise to more and more independent thinkers, Africa's numerous cultural systems and cosmologies may serve as a healthy reminder to the aggressive followers of the Abrahamic tradition and their communist rivals that the future civilization of this planet is going to be based on three major elements: namely, the spirit of cultural tolerance, the scientific spirit of enquiry, and the Abrahamic spirit of communion with the Ruler of the Visible Kingdom of Matter and the Invisible Kingdom of Spirit. In this human attempt at modern civilization-building, the African contribution to the banquet of civilizations will be the capacity for suffering, the capability to co-exist in a highly diverse cultural world, and the unflagging belief in the spiritual continuity of physical life. These three major contributions will be added to the American, European, Latin American, and Asiatic contributions to lay the foundations of the emerging universal technological civilization.

1

INTRODUCTION TO TRADITIONAL AFRICAN COSMOLOGY

*T*raditional Africa was, and still is, rich in cosmological ideas. Though the diversity of Africa's religious and cosmological heritage has been little known outside of the continent, the intensive researches of Africanists around the world and the growing global interest in the African world have combined to draw attention to what could be Africa's spiritual gift to humanity. This gift is less understood by many Africans, and even much less by the greater majority of non-Africans.

Africa's traditional cosmology is diverse, as I already pointed out above; but behind this diversity lies the core of shared beliefs which spread across the continent. This study does not plan to bring out the differences; rather it seeks to construct a framework of analysis out of the body of ideas that researchers in the field have agreed upon as the common elements in the various cosmological systems among African's numerous ethnic groups.

A. 1. The Traditional African Conception of Man

In the cosmological world of traditional African man, certain ideas have always held sway over men's minds. The idea of a Deity who rules over creation was accepted by many, if not most, African peoples. In fact, African pioneers in the field of traditional African religion, such as Professors Idowu and Mbiti, have informed us that this African knowledge of God is expressed in proverbs, short statements, prayers, names, stories, myths, and religious ceremonies.[13] Dr. Mbiti believes that a careful examination of these sources of African religious beliefs would bring out the unity in diversity which characterizes the traditional African world of religion. He makes this point clearly in the following passage:

> "It is remarkable that in spite of great distances separating the peoples of one region from those of another, there are sufficient elements of belief which make it possible for us to discuss African concepts of God as a unity and on a continental scale.[14]

This Divine Creator is usually pictured as the Lord and Maker of mankind. In the numerous myths of African peoples, such as those of the Yoruba, the Ashanti, the Dogon, and others, we learn that in the beginning God was very close to mankind; but later as a result of man's provocation, error or folly, God withdrew and so man forfeited his privileges and benefits to be in close proximity to his Creator.

All these mythological ideas, from which we deduce the African conception of God and his relations to mankind, do help us in understanding the traditional African's definition of self vis-a-vis the Supreme Being. Judging from the accounts provided in the writings of students of African religion, there is a close and intimate relationship between man and the Supreme Being. According to this view, man is indeed more than a spectator on the stage of life. Though he is a creature who is circumscribed within the parameters set by the spiritual world of the Supreme Being, the lesser divinities, the departed ancestors and the evil spirits, he still exercises his own will on both the material and spiritual worlds. For man to function effectively in the material world, he must indeed learn to pursue his human needs and personal interests without antagonizing the spiritual forces above him.

Man, in traditional African cosmology, is caught in a triangular matrix of spiritual relationships. There are first the unbreakable ties to the Supreme Being, who created the earth and everything therein for man and his progeny. These ties are unbreakable because man's existence is ontologically dependent upon his Creator. Secondly, man has also to maintain correct relationship with the lesser entities within the spiritual kingdom. His day-to-day activities are not only designed to harmonize his relationship with the divinities and the departed ancestors, but they are also motivated by the fear that bad relations with these spiritual forces could certainly endanger the life and safety of his community. This, then, brings us to the third point concerning man's triangular relationship with the spiritual world.

In the cosmological scheme of traditional African man, the fusion of the profane and the sacred has implications for the relations between the individual and the spiritual world, as well as the individual and his community. The African traditional religionist believes that any violation of behavioral and ritual codes constitutes a betrayal to one's soul and to one's community.

This understanding of the triangular relationship between the individual and his community, on the one hand, and the spiritual kingdom on the other, puts a premium on good behavior and obedience to communal customs and practices. This sense of obedience and harmony hinges upon man's realization that the universe is a religious one, and everything within it dances to a cosmic music whose tune and rhythm echo the words of the spiritual forces. In other words, African traditional man learns to be obedient and religious all the time, simply because he knows fully well that the cosmic order abhors the disrespectors of religious commands and rituals. Life, according to this traditional African man, is a constant dialogue with the sacred, and each passing moment demands our utmost devotion to the spiritual forces above, and to the words of religious communication issuing from their invisible lips. It is because of this constant dialogue with the spiritual world around him that the traditional African conceives himself as the centerpiece of creation. John Mbiti captures this aspect of traditional Africa's ontology when he writes:

> "...African ontology is basically anthropo-centric; man is at the very centre of existence, and African peoples see everything else as its relation to this central position of man. God is the explanation of man's origin and sustenance; it is as if God exists for the sake of man. The spirits are ontologically in the mode between God and man; they describe or explain the destiny of man after physical life.[15]

This African conception of the Homo/Deus relationship is radically different from the orthodox Semitic religions wherein man is generally looked upon as an abject sinner who must submit to God in order to deserve his mercy and grace in the Hereafter. In fact, some segments within the Abrahamic tradition confidently believe that man is created *only* to serve God, and his acts of disobedience and unrighteousness will inevitably land him in the fires of hell.

Another point that deserves some emphasis here is the fact that the traditional African sees the universe as a hierarchy of vital forces, and man is that force which links the inanimate objects to the world of the spiritual forces above him. This aspect of the traditional African conception of man makes us see man as both a manipulator of spiritual power and as a target of such a power. Because of this understanding of reality, the traditional African's view of man, especially as characterized in Bantu philosophy, has been described as vitalistic; that is, it is based upon the belief that life is a vital unity and that the human being is only a point on the cosmic circle of life. This view, when analyzed carefully, leads us to say with Reverend Vincent Mulago that:

> The common factor which explains the solidarity of clan or tribe is not at all simple. It is not the life of the senses, nor the life of thought. Neither is it life in the multicolored diversity we find in newspapers or in the modern novel. It is life as it has been derived and received from the source of "power," as it turns toward power, is seized by it and seizes it. This life is not destroyed by death, although death may subject it to a change of condition.[16]

This understanding of man, as described by Reverend Mulago's statement, is very much related to Father Tempels' formulations in his *Bantu Philosophy*. In this widely quoted but controversial work, Father Tempels tries to give philosophical bearing to what seems to him to be the simple and natural Bantu understanding of reality and the Supreme Being. He identifies the supreme value in African thought as vital-force and he claims that the end of the whole range of African man's activities is "to acquire life, strength or vital force, to live strongly, that they are to make life stronger, or to assume that force shall remain perpetually in one's posterity."[17]

Reverend Mulago, in a paper written for a consultation conference of Christian theologians in 1966, took the same line of reasoning as Father Tempels, when he argued that "For the Bantu, living is existence in community, it is participation in the sacred life (and all life is sacred) of the ancestors; it is an extension of the life of one's forefathers, and a preparation for one's own life to be carried on in one's descendants."[18]

This statement of Mulago is generally accepted by all students of African traditional religion as a standard belief among Africans. It is, however, noteworthy to point out in passing that Mulago's article has improved upon Father Temple's work. In fact, his claim that vital participation "is the main if not the only basis of all their (Bantu peoples he studied) family, social, political and religious institutions and customs," has given us an alternative method to that of the Flemmish priest. Dr. Mulago certainly adds to our understanding of the Bantu view of man when he tells us that "The Bantu view of life may be seen in two ways: first, as a community of blood (the main primary factor); and secondly, as a community or property (the concomitant factor which makes life possible.")[19]

This view of man is a fairly adequate statement of what the majority of traditional African religionists would accept. It not only shows that African man believes in the sacred perpetuation of the powers of procreation in his line of descent, but it also articulates the universal belief that all the non-human elements in nature (trees, animals and inorganic beings) are the extensions and means of life of those to whom they belong. This African view of life is the basis for the African fear of impotency among men and barrenness among women. Such human mishaps and existential woes are construed by traditional African man as the severing of the chain of being, linking the living and the dead. In the view of traditional African man, the link between ancestors and their present successors on earth comes from the unity of blood and the common life which circulates in the veins, of all the members of the community.[20]

In addition to the points mentioned above we should also take note of Janheinz Jahn's efforts to reconstruct Bantu philosophy. In his interesting book *Muntu*, Jahn identified three elements which he felt were basic to African thought. The first and second of these three elements in his list are similar to what we have already learned from Father Tempels and Dr. Mulago. Jahn's contribution to our understanding of traditional African view of life and of man's role in the process of vital participation is his claim that one of the touchstones of traditional African culture is the "magic power of the word." Writing on this aspect of Jahn's formulation of Bantu thought, Claude Wauthier says:

> Jahn equates this (the word) with Nommo of Dogon Cosmogony, which is 'word, water, seed and blood' all at once, according to Ogotemeli, the sage whom Griaule questioned. In African metaphysics, as Jahn explains them, 'all transformations, creation and procreation is made by the word,' which is also the life force and controlled only by the Muntu.[21]

The truth about this formulation of Jahn is not widely disputed, for as Wauthier himself noted, the word is all-powerful in Africa. Indeed, we can also add that the traditional African religionists of old did not only take words seriously, but they also saw language both as the badge of man's spiritual superiority over the non-human elements in the universe and as his shibboleth at the spiritual gates of the Supreme Being's invisible Kingdom.

This traditional African view of the magical power of words is evident in the many references by scholars to the African's use of incantations in his day-to-day living. This belief in the magic power of words gave rise to specialization in the execution of functions in many traditional African societies. The caste system, for example, emerged in certain societies in Africa simply because the African peoples felt that such a division of labour could bring about a good relationship with the spiritual world, and that the human elements so chosen for such functions could execute their delicate and sensitive tasks without endangering the lives of others in the community.

Hampate Ba, in commenting on the nature of African art, has argued that the African conception of art will not be intelligible to a person who is secularistic in his understanding of reality, for such an art is inspired by a world-view that is all-embracing and religious. He further contends that, in the old Africa, "Every act and every gesture were considered to bring into play the invisible forces of life. According to the tradition of the Bambara people of Mali, these forces are the multiple aspects of SE or Great Creative Power, which is itself an aspect of the Supreme Being known as Maa Ngala."[22]

To return to Janheinz Jahn's formulations of Bantu philosophy, we can now conclude with him that in African thought in general and Bantu thought in particular:

> God is either a creator, a planner; or he is universal begetter, the pure force of procreation, the primal phallus of a spermatic religion, as Sartre affirms or he is, as the philosophy itself would suggest, Ntu itself, and that would mean: that Being which is at once force and mother, unseparated and undivided, sleeping primal force, yet without nommo, without 'life.'[23]

With this understanding we can now conclude this section of the chapter. But before proceeding to the other portions of this study, let us recapitulate the main points and then use them as points of departure for the next section. The chief points could be summarized as follows: (1) that the traditional African man sees himself in a hierarchy of cosmic beings; (2) that his status and position in such a scheme is one of privilege, although he is still open to dangers from both the spiritual and physical worlds; (3) that his existence is dependent on the process of vital participation in the communion of the living and the non-living; (4) that his life is a marriage between spirit and matter; and (5) that he must always remember that the demarcation line between the visible and the invisible worlds is a very thin one.

A.2. The African View of Man's Destiny

In the traditional African man's ontological system the human being is given a definite destiny. Though the details about the nature of this destiny vary from group to group, the fact remains that in the old Africa man was viewed as a cosmic traveller who is destined to cross the equator of death. This boundary line between the living and the departed is what gives meaning to life itself, for, just like the equator, it serves as a demarcation line between two inseparable portions of total reality. This is to say, death in the view of old Africa is "not the ultimate reality but life. At death the individual dissolves into collective immortality of the living-dead, that is, proclaims the great solidarity of life."[24]

The above statement clearly shows that, to the traditional African religionist, death is the process and the condition by which the physical body of man is disintegrated. It is also the fragmentation of the unity of life: body and spirit.

From the above understanding we can also say with Reverend Mbiti that, "Death is conceived of as a departure and not a complete annihilation of a person. He moves on to join the company of the departed, and the only major change is the decay of the physical body, but the spirit moves on to another state of existence."[25]

This passing away of the soul from the physical world of man (or Muntu, to borrow a Bantu term), though a phase in the human pilgrimage to the spiritual kingdom of the unseen, is a very complex and paradoxical matter. Indeed, its paradoxical and complex nature has given rise to different myths about its origins and significance. E.G. Parrinder, for example, had written in connection with the soul and its destiny, that "the complexity of African ideas is so great that some peoples have belief in at least five distinguishable powers in man."[26] Though Parrinder fails to list the five powers in man, we have learned from Father Tempels that "the dead live on in a diminished condition of life, as lessened life forces, while retaining their higher, strengthening fathering life force."[27] This is to say that the departed, by going through the individualized agony of death, have gained in deeper knowledge of the mystery and the process of vital participation in the Universe.

These aspects of death are made complicated because of the manner in which man's destiny is conceived by Africa's diverse groups. Among the Kinyaruanda Bantus, Reverend Kagame tells us, there are three words meaning life. They are *Bugingo, Buzima,* and *Magara.* Bugingo means the duration of life; buzima means the union of a shadow with a body; and magara is the spiritual life of a man. These three concepts are very important in our understanding of the Bantu conception of man's destiny. First of all, we should note that, as an abstraction, the word buzima falls under the category called Kuntu, the category of way or manner.

After having improved upon the concepts he borrowed from Kagame, Jaheinz Jahn concluded that the origin of a human being is a double process because, on the one hand, it is the biological union of shadow and body according to the principle buzima; and on the other, it is a spiritual unity of the body with Nommo-force. The principle which designates the union of Nommo-force with a body is called *Magara:* life.[28]

Because of this Bantu view of man, Kagame himself concludes that Bantu philosophy knows of the problem of immortality and has recognized and solved it long ago. He adds that the African likes to continue living forever. But since death is inevitable, he decides to prolong his existence through his descendants. This desire to be immortal is so prominent in the hierarchy of African ideas of existence that death is always reluctantly accepted, and quite frequently attributed to some external causes.

This paradoxical understanding of death has led many African peoples to explain death as the result of four causes. The most commonly cited cause is magic, sorcery and witchcraft. This cause is viewed by most Africans as a very dangerous one, for victims of such evil practices may turn out to be wandering ghosts whose souls will not be at rest.

The second cause of death is the curse. Many African societies teach their new members that a powerful curse brings immediate death to the accursed. Such a fate is widely feared in African traditional societies, and every precaution is usually taken not to violate taboos, customs and traditions. The third cause of death is the living-dead. These departed souls may be dissatisfied with the life and activities of their survivors on earth and so decide to tell them to change their ways by visiting them with calamities. Though this possible cause of death is held by some of Africa's ethnic groups, the fact still remains that there is little evidence that the living-dead actually cause death.

The fourth cause of death is God. This category of death includes only those that are difficult to explain. They range from death through lightning to the natural passing away of old people. This category is not rigid, however. The traditional African may accept God as the ultimate cause of death, but to satisfy his psychological and emotional needs he still would insist on intermediate causes of death.

These four causes of death together could affect the destiny of a man. If indeed a man dies as a result of black magic, his soul would not rest in peace, and the ontological transformation which is the result of death would also remain unfulfilled. It is, of course, this fear of one's post-mortem lot that drives many an African into the arms of the diviners and magicians. These mediators between fragile and vulnerable men and the spiritual powers are practitioners of great knowledge in the mystical arts, and their ability to allay the fears of their clients and to subdue their real or imagined targets has contributed a great deal to African social stability in the past. These qualities have also guaranteed the peaceful passage of man from the realm of human to the world of spirits.

A. 3. African Understanding of History

It has been said by John S. Mbiti that African ontology is a religious one and that "the key to our understanding of the basic religious and philosophical concepts, is the African concept of time." He went on to argue that, "according to traditional African concepts, time is a two-dimensional phenomenon, with a long past, a present and virtually no future."[29]

These formulations of Mbiti have given currency to the view that, to the old Africa, history consists of two parts, namely the Sasa and the Zamani. The Sasa is composed of all the events which in western or linear concept of time would be considered as the future. This concept, in the writings of Mbiti, is taken as that dimension which embraces all events that are about to occur or are in the process of occurring or have recently occurred. It is also understood as the most meaningful period of the individual.

Zamani, on the other hand, is described by Mbiti as the macro-time, which embraces all the past events that link the beginning of things to the present unfolding of events in the universe. In his view, Zamani is more than the past; it is as he suggests, "the graveyard of time." Zamani, therefore, is not only the period of termination, but also the period of myth.

The conceptual scheme of Mbiti does help us understand the particularisms of African thought, but it certainly will not be the last word in the debate over the African concept of history. Although I believe that Mbiti has done a good job in bringing out to the western world, in a language they can understand, the intellectual and religious fruits of Africa's non-literate sages of yesteryears, I also think J.N.K. Mugambi was correct when he wrote, in 1974, that Mbiti's linguistic basis for his conclusions on the absence of indefinite future in African thought is too simplistic. There is definitely some truth in this point. Indeed, though much research needs to be done on the matter, we can assert here that Mugambi is quite correct in saying that:

> To assert that Africans do not conceive of a future beyond two years . . .
> is to imply in the same assertion that Africans do not have any traditional
> means or principles by which they ensure a perpetuation of their
> communities.[30]

After presenting Mbiti's interpretation of the African conception of history, let me offer briefly an alternative conceptual scheme while drawing on the same findings of Mbiti and others in the field. As suggested in our discussion on the nature of African traditional man, the African's view of the destiny of man is that of a gradual and peaceful transition from the human to the spiritual world. This idea of a transition suggests to me that man must be conceptualized differently from what we have heard from scholars like Mbiti and Idowu.

In my view, the key concept in traditional African thought is the cosmic schizophrenic tendencies of man. By this I mean that traditional African man sees himself as a citizen of three different worlds at the same time. This is to say that he lives in (a) the world of concrete reality, (b) the world of social values, and (c) the world of ineffable self-consciousness. The first world is that of man, trees, stars, inanimate objects and phenomena. The second is that of values governing the mental and spiritual processes of man and his community. The third is the world of unreachable and inexpressible spiritual powers.

When we analyze carefully the beliefs and thought patterns of traditional African man we find that these could be fitted into the three major ontological categories. The tendency of some of the students of African religions to assert that Africans do not worship one God is due to this cosmic schizophrenic behavior in man. In the African concept, traditional man places the High God in the world of ineffable self-conscious. Though he shuttles between this particular world and the other two, his ontological makeup seems to incline him more to the realms of concrete reality and social values respectively. This is to say that traditional African man's view of history is different from that of the ascetic religious traditions of the East, where man renounces this earthly life and devotes his entire life and being to the world of ineffable self-consciousness. The African view is also different from the western scientific view, which focuses almost completely on the world of concrete reality. The western view, it should be added, is based on the dynamics of matter and its conception of time and history is bound to be affected by the changing paradigms in the scientific community of the West.[31]

As long as western man hankers after the mysteries of matter his concept of time will be unilinear. In other words, the conception of time of a human group is determined more by the ontological focus of its members (that is, which of the three worlds they wish to choose) and less by an inherent racial or geographical factor. In fact, the ontological focus of activities is the cause and the effect of the series of preferences associated with a particular society. A society conceives time in the manner of old Africa because in such a society the ontological focus is on the world of social values. This world, which is the sum of values governing the meanings, and interrelationships between ontological units, is paramount in African thought because all the other worlds of which man is a citizen are subject to the world of social values. To put this in another way, I would say that in traditional African thought, the need for harmony between man and God, man and man, and man and the non-human elements in the universe has led to an ontological emphasis on the world of social values. As a result of such an overemphasis, traditional Africa held supreme the traditions of the ancients (ancestors). It is this overemphasis on the sources of traditions and customs that misled Mbiti to deny the African a sense of indefinite future.

Contrary to Mbiti, I would argue that African traditional man indeed has a sense of the definite future, but that his ontological focus has been not in revolutionizing the physical landscape around him, but on socializing the new members of society to anticipate their successful accession to fatherhood (which is a few years hence) and to refresh their memory of past events. This latter aspect of the African response to the ontological challenge put a premium on the retrieval facilities of the mind and its memory. This ontological response, more than any other thing, is responsible for the African's late adoption of what Ali A. Mazrui calls "the technology of intellectual conversation." The fact that Africans

are not naturally inferior intellectually has been proven by the large
number of students from Africa who came from non-literate families
and yet earned first class degrees from major western universities,
where the great-grandchildren of European literates failed to make a
better performance.

These African success stories are categorical denials of the racial
inferiority usually associated with Africa's children. My view is that the
traditional African's conception of history, and his continent's material
underdevelopment were the effects of his ontological response rather
than the confirmations of his genetic deficiency.

In light of the above reasoning I would now conclude that the
traditional African man's concept of time is three-dimensional. This is
to say that he believes in a past, a present and a future. Yet, in conceding
this point, I need to add that the matter does not end with the three-
dimensionality of time. The nature of such a conception needs further
exploration; but because I have neither the time nor the space of explore
these frontiers of African thought, I find it appropriate to make two
observations concerning its nature. First of all, it should be pointed out
that the concept of unilinearity of time, as developed in western history,
is based on an illusion. The illusion is indetectable so long as man chases
after the mirage of materiality. This illusion becomes exposed the
moment the ontological response of a society shifts its focus from
excessive love for materiality to excessive love for the social values and
relationships between men in society.

To put this great philosophical point over which African man differs
substantially with his western counterpart in another way, I would like
to argue that, whereas the western theory of historical unilinearity is
inspired by the matrix of causes and effects that govern the world of
concrete reality, the African's conception of time is guided by his
excessive concern for communal harmony in rituals, deeds and
thoughts.

The idea of unilinearity of history is inspired by, and based on, the
intercourse between the various elements in the hierarchical order of
ontological units in the universe. These two visions of history and life
are very different indeed, and only a fool would absolutize the concept
of unilinearity as developed out of one experience and then try desperately to impose it on the rest of mankind.

In summarizing the foregoing discussion I think it is worth noting that the African's concept of the triangular relationship between God, man and the non-human elements in the universe is the key to the understanding of traditional African philosophy. This view, as we have seen above, does not only shed light on the self-image of African man, but it also provides us with an intellectual map of the metaphysical world of the traditional African man.

Another conclusion to be drawn from the foregoing discussion is that traditional African man sees himself as a party to an ontological and cosmological partnership and, because of this understanding of his life on earth, he always sees harmony as the best form of human expression. To the traditional African man, life is chaotic so long as man's links with God and others in existence are shattered. Because of this fear of breaking the ontological bonds, traditional African man always prefers harmony and social order.

In addition to the above, one can also conclude that African cosmology sees history not as a series of discontinuities which reflect man's exercise of the promethean will, but as an ever growing chain of being, whose beginning is the act of Divine creation and whose end is the recession of the dead man's spirit into the realm of immortality. When this traditional African undertanding of man's destiny is closely examined we cannot but conclude that, to the traditional African man, an act is historically significant only when it perpetuates his line of descent and immortalizes memories about his earthly life.

2

THE ISLAMIC INVASION OF THE AFRICAN WORLD

The Islamic religion is now a major factor in human life and its impact is felt not only in Arabia, where it started out and then spread to the four corners of the earth, embracing a significant portion of humanity, but also in Africa where it has in many cases displaced an indigenous belief system whose world view, though similar to Islam in certain respects, varies widely from it.

This section of the chapter deals with the Islamic world view. It does not only seek to elucidate the most salient and very important points about the Islamic faith, but it also wishes to provide the reader with background information so that he can, after having read the first part of this study, reach a better understanding of the difference between traditional African thought and orthodox Islamic thought.

A. 1. The Islamic View of Life

By way of an introduction I would begin by saying that the religion of Islam holds that man is a creature of God (Allah), that his life on earth is of a fixed duration, and that his deeds, activities and thoughts, while living in the community of men, will all be scrutinized and judged in the hereafter by the Best of all Judges (Allah).[31] The Islamic concept of man emphasizes, *inter alia,* three important things about him: namely, his finitude, his dependency upon Allah, and his judgement. To orthodox Muslims, Allah is the Creator who created each and every individual man for a fixed time. During his lifetime this creature is expected to serve and worship his Maker. The Holy Quran says that since the creation of Adam, mankind had been blessed with a chain of messengers bearing the Divine instructions on how to live and worship Him on this earth. It further states that Allah had seen to it that every nation and people in history was provided with Divine guidance, and that the process came to a glorious end only with the emergence and departure from this world of the Holy Prophet Muhammad. Hence, his title of Khatam Al-Nabiin (The seal of the Prophets).[33]

Because of this Quranic understanding of the Divine plan for man on earth, Muslims teach their young ones to remember at all times the brevity of life and the sweetness of the hereafter. This strong emphasis on devotion to Allah and things eternal has been taken more seriously by the Sufi sects in Islam. Their adherence to the doctrine that this life is ephemeral and that the Hereafter is better, derives from the constant and solemn Quranic reiteration of this fact, and many of their numbers have found solace and joy on earth only in their soul-searching and endless attempts to be *in the presence of their Creator.* Those in Islam who are not too mystical in their rituals and conceptions of the teachings of Islam have tended to be Muslims whose orthodox beliefs and practices are carried out on the surface of life. Theirs is a world of activities whose processes and actions are consciously or unconsciously guided by the beliefs, rituals and ideas enjoined upon men by the Quran.

The finitude of man, therefore, is one of the main points emphasized throughout the Quran. In Suratul Asr, man is reminded that "by the token of time through the ages, he has been a loser." Allah elaborates upon this theme of human folly by stressing to man that only those with faith and good deeds are winners. He concludes this short Surah by saying that such blessed achievements are obtained by men who are patient, persevering, and truthful.[34] In another Surah, Allah makes it categorically clear that those who believe and do good deeds are the *best of creatures*, (Hairul Bariyat); on the other hand, those who do not believe and do evil deeds are the worst of creatures, (Sharul Bariyat).[35]

The brevity of life on earth is known to all men, and Allah in the Quran cites numerous natural and physical phenomena to teach mankind about the finitude that is its lot. The Quran asks us to consider the dry earth which Allah converts every rainy season from an empty field into a vast area covered with green grass from one end to the other. Yet this beautiful grass field could easily be transformed once again into a dry wasteland without any sign of plant life. These variations in the weather and in the life of the plant kingdom, the Quran teaches, are just examples of Allah's power over what our scientists now call the world of nature.

These phenomena we observe daily in the world around us are all signs of Allah, and the Quran advises man to reflect on them; for by supplementing his faith with reflections on the wonders of creation, he stands to gain a lot spiritually. Such exercises do not only raise his level of spiritual consciousness, but they also enable him to see in the changing phenomena of this world the vague outlines of the Divine

Truths he is searching for in his inner self. But since man's life is short and is also ridden with mistakes and errors, he has to cling to Allah for guidance and protection against evil in all its forms in the universe. Without Divine guidance mankind is eternally lost; and without revelation, life for humanity is action without reflection and meaning. Because of this weakness in the human condition man has to acknowledge his dependency; but interestingly enough, such a state of dependency is paradoxically best expressed in man's assumed and acknowledged dominance in the material universe. To put this rather contradictory fact in another way, I should say that man's superiority over all other factors in the material universe is the most glaring illustration of his weakness. Man, I should also add here, is that being whose dominance and superiority have conspired to confer upon him the mantle of dependency, not of self-sufficiency.

Unlike the African cosmologist who sees a man's life as a link in a chain of beings going back to a mystical founder of his clan or tribe, the Muslim orthodox theologian sees himself as an existential unit who is endowed by Allah with an appointed time to go through the challenges of life. This privileged creature is not by any means responsible for the deeds of his predecessors; nor are they responsible for his. His life has nothing to do ontologically and theologically with the lives of his progeny, and all their deeds will be judged separately, not collectively. This is to say that Islam holds every man responsible for his deeds, and that on the Day of Judgement justice will be meted out according to one's deeds, and not on the basis of one's ancestry or birth.

The Quranic teaching on the hereafter is so emphatic that no devout Muslim would have any doubt about it. Allah has mentioned in several Quranic verses (ayats) that man's life on earth is a brief one, that each creature will be called to account when the world comes to an end, and that the Day of Judgement is inevitable. Because of this Quranic concern about the Last Day of life on earth, many vivid and attractive descriptions of Heaven and Hell are given in the Quran. Man is given firm and categorical promise of a blissful paradise if only he obeys and serves Allah while on earth. He is equally warned not to do evil in this life, or punishment and torment will await him beyond the grave.

To sum up this discussion on the Islamic view of life, one can say that, contrary to traditional African thought, Islamic theology sees man as a privileged creature who is given trust on earth by the Divine; that is to say, he is called upon to serve as the Viceregent of Allah on earth, and to account for each and every deed of his life in this sublunary world.[36] Another point of importance in the Islamic belief system about man and his destiny is that, although life is short and full of evil, man should take heart in the fact that there is life beyond the grave. This promise of a hereafter is a major difference between Islam and traditional African thought, which generally pays less attention to the details of a hereafter. As already noted in the first section of this study, the traditional African cosmologist focuses primarily on the dead man's post-mortem relations with his family, his clan, his tribe, and the fellow humans who have survived him. To put this in another way, one could say that old Africa believed that immortality was obtained through the acts of respect shown to departed ancestors by the community of the living, or through the gradual recession of the dead ancestor into the realm of the spirits.

Last but not least, on this subject, one could argue that the Islamic view of man sees him as a creature whose destiny is determined both by himself and by his Maker. The Quran has addressed numerous warnings to rebellious mankind not to go astray; and it is also known for its announcement that the last days of the earth are ones in which our Lord will certainly bring to justice all those men who have taken no note of man's finitude, his dependency and his judgement before Allah.

A.2. The Islamic Penetration of Africa

The advent of Islam in Africa was a result of the rapid sweep the Muslim armies were making in the early decades of the Islamic movement. Though Africans had contacts with Arabians prior to the rise of Islam,[38] the fact remains that Africa's territorial integrity and her peoples' destiny were never threatened by Arabians. Such a possibility became a reality only when Egypt fell into their hands.

The harbinger of the Muslim victory in Africa was 'Amr Ibn Al-As, a Muslim commander who saw the Muslim victory over the Byzantines in Syria as a signal to the Muslims. This act of 'Amr Ibn Al-As opened the doors of Africa to Arab military power and cultural influence.

Soon the Arab armies began to march across the continent in search of new kingdoms and new opportunities for themselves. Those who came as military governors founded towns and villages, which later became the basis of urban life and culture in the Northern part of Africa. To these Arab immigrants from the East this part of Africa was comparable to the new frontier of the Americas in later years and every enterprising fellow in the Islamic world saw the Western part of Daral-Islam as the Maghrib.[39]

The conquest of the Maghrib gave rise to two processes, namely, Arabization and Islamization. The first process proved successful because Arabic was the language of government and trade. Because it was the language of the conquistadores from the East, it gradually gained ground, owing to its prestige and usefulness.

One of the most interesting factors which assisted in the realization of the second process, mentioned above, is the mercantile community. These merchants, who came from as far as Persia (Iran) to conduct business, were bent on gaining a foothold in the centers of civilization in the Maghrib. It was, therefore, in this role that they made a meaningful contribution to the Islamization of this region of Africa. In light of this understanding one could say that this intermingling of peoples and cultures actually paved the way for the gradual penetration of Islam into the Maghrib.

When Islam conquered Egypt, the western part of North Africa was inhabited by the Berbers. This large ethnic group, which was then occupying the mountains and plains of the area as well as the Sahara, was divided into three major groupings, Lowata, Sanhaja, and Zanata, each subdivided into a great number of smaller tribes. Prior to Islam the majority of these groups remained outside the cultural orbit of the powerful civilizations that dotted the shores of North Africa. Though ancient historians gave us some account about the subservient relationship between these Berbers and the Phoenicians, Greeks, Carthaginians, Romans and Byzantines, who came over as conquerors and traders, the fact remains that, up to the time of the Islamic conquest, the Berbers enjoyed a high degree of political freedom. They came under Arab rule only after much struggle and blood. E. W. Bovill, in describing this crucial period in North African history, captured this fact when he wrote:

> Just when the Arab triumph seemed complete the Berbers' passionate love of liberty gave birth to one of those supreme national efforts, which, at the moment of crises, have so often saved the conquered from extinction.[40]

Despite their heroic resistance to Arab domination of North Africa, the Berbers gradually lost ground to these invaders from the East. They succeeded only in keeping the highlands, which proved too difficult for the Arabs to attack and take over.

The Arab triumph in North Africa was a result of a series of raids by commanders from the East. The most historically significant invasion took place in the middle of the eleventh century when the members of the Banu Hilal and Sulaim fell on the Maghrib. The atrocities perpetrated by these tribes sent a shock wave throughout the length and breadth of the area. Much arable land was destroyed and many of the Berbers, for the first time in their national history, came directly under Arab dynasties and rulers.

The decision of these tribes to settle down in the Maghrib led to the intermarriage and cultural fusion that took place between certain groups in North Africa and the Arabs. The process of Arabization gained limited momentum as a result of the mass exodus of Arab tribesmen from the East. Many of these men settled down in urban areas and hence intermarried with Berber women. This integration of families of Arabs and Berbers made it possible for Islam to grow and spread.

The growth of Arab power, be it noted, did not mean the total collapse of Berber resistance. To the contrary; the processes or Arabization and Islamization were accompanied for several decades by violence and coercion. In fact, so unstable and rebellious were the Berbers that they "apostatized twelve times before Islam gained a firm foothold over them."[41]

When the Berbers finally succumbed to Islam the Muslims in the Maghrib began to build up a major civilization in the area. This process was made possible, and in part accelerated, by the constant passing of men and ideas from the East to the Far West (al-Maghrib Al-Aqsa). These new arrivals from the East were pioneers who were in search of adventure. Many passed through the Maghrib on their way to Andalusia, which was already conquered by the Arabs in collaboration with Berbers and other Africans from Maghrib.

This conquest of Spain was very significant for, as Bovill noted in his *The Golden Trade of the Moors,* the transaction flow between the Maghrib Muslims and their brethren in the Andalusian country helped keep them well-posted with the great achievements of their fellows in Europe. Such a transaction flow made Morocco a vital link in the chain which bound eastern and western Islam. From the East came scholars,

merchants, and craftsmen seeking a share in the wealth and culture of
the West. Bovill captured the mood of the day when he wrote the
following passage:-

> From Spain there was a ceaseless flow of the oppressed, victims of
> political and religious persecution, and fugitives from justice; most of
> them were skilled agriculturists, but many erudite scholars were of their
> numbers. Thus was the Maghrib al-Aqsa nourished by two converging
> streams of fresh and invigorating blood. How richly their confluence
> blessed the country is strikingly illustrated by the city of Fez.[42]

With the growth of this Islamic civilization in Morocco, ideas and
wares began to flow to the south of the Sahara. This trade between the
Maghrib and the sub-Saharan peoples, which many historians believe to
have existed prior to the advent of Islam in the area, must have been of
great benefit to Morocco. Bernard Lewis has suggested that the two
most important Moroccan exports to the East at this time were gold and
slaves, and that when the Berbers became Muslims the rulers felt it
necessary to find alternative sources of slaves. This alternative source of
supply was found in the still unconquered lands to the south, and Muslim
merchants from the Mediterranean coast travelled for months to reach
the trading centers of Ghana, where gold and slaves were easily
obtainable.[43]

These merchants were to a certain extent responsible for the spread
of Islam in the Sahara, because it was through their constant peddling of
goods from both Maghrib and the Sudan that they succeeded in impress-
ing upon the Africans the beauty and simplicity of their faith. These
merchants, however, were not primarily interested in propagating
Islam; they came to the south mainly to make money and to buy at a
very low price. It was not until later that they set out deliberately to win
converts, and then it was largely a Berber affair.

The Berbers seemed to have been chosen by history to carry the
banner of Islam into West Africa, because of their geographical loca-
tion and their historical role as middle-men between Arabs and black
Africans. The first Berber tribe in the Sahara to play a major role in the
Islamization process was the Sanhaja. This ethnic group became Muslim
as a result of their interaction with the Muslim traders who had settled
in their midst. One result of the Sanhaja conversion to Islam was the
performance of the Hajj by their rulers.

This process went on for many years until Yahia ibn Ibrahim, a Sanhaja Paramount Chief who was passing through Kairawan on his way from Mecca, asked Abu Amran to help him secure the services of someone who could teach him and his subjects about the religion of Islam. This search for a teacher resulted in the selection of Ibn Yasin, a fanatical instructor whose austere doctrine proved unbearable to Yahia's people. In response to their act of rejection of austere doctrine, Abdulla Ibn Yasin set off towards the Sudan borderland.[44] He founded a fortified fraternity center (ribat) somewhere near the Atlantic coast. This center quickly turned into a war camp and Ibn Yasin wasted no time in conquering his enemies. It was indeed the series of successes enjoyed by his followers that made their name famous. The Almoravids went down in history as a major religious movement whose activities and successes, though short-lived, helped in bringing many people into the fold of Islam.

The rise of the Almoravids did not only mean the fanatical propagation of Islam in the Sahara, but it also opened the door to greater contact between the Berbers and the Africans to the South. This interaction, which was beneficial to the dissemination of the Islamic religion, was conflictive in many respects, because both parties found it politically and strategically useful to keep each other in check. So preoccupied were those two parties with such a power play that each was ready to attack the other. The Sanhaja Berbers were quick to realize that Islam could be a useful tool with which to rally and organize themselves. The historical evidence seems to point out that such politically astute decisions were taken only under circumstances of grave danger, and that the most interesting example which is directly related to our discussion of early Islam in the Sahara and the West of Sudan is that which occurred at about 1020 A.D. This act of unity by the different Berber tribes was motivated by their collective desire to bring down the Ghanaian Kingdom. In fact, this much-needed unity which the Lemtuna, Godala and Masufa Berbers hoped for, was based on the ideas acquired by one of their leaders, Tarsina the Lemtune, whose pilgrimage to Mecca inspired him to rationalize his campaigns against black Africans in the name of the Islamic Jihad.

Added to this political calculation was also the fact that "these Atlantic Berbers were feeling hemmed in between the Zanata who had gained control of the Moroccan oases and ruled from Sijilmasa and the powerful black kingdom of Ghana which had captured Awadaghast, their south Saharan center."[45] The insecurity of these Berber groups led to much conflict between them and the sources of their fears and apprehension - the Kingdom of Ghana.

The Kingdom of Ghana collapsed only after the Almoravids were successfully organized in the name of Islam. With their Islamically oriented organization these Atlantic Berbers embarked on a campaign to win converts by force of arms. After many years of planning and organization the Berbers, under the leadership of Abu Bakr, finally managed in 1076 to seize control of the capital of Ghana, Kumbi. This triumph of the Berbers led to the massacre of the inhabitants of the city and the subjection of the whole country to a form of Berber imperialism based on Islam.

"The consequences of this Almoravid conquest," E. W. Bovill has told us, "were not as far-reaching as might have been expected, because the collapse of the Almoravids in the south was even more rapid than in the north."[46] What Bovill wished to say was that, with the destruction of their common enemy (Ghana) the Atlantic Berbers, particularly the Godala and the Masufa, soon found themselves at each other's throats. This growing disunity within the Berber ranks finally led to the end of Almoravid hegemony in 1087.

Such a rapid decline in the power of the Almoravids paved the way for the liberation of the peoples of Ghana. In fact, little more than a decade after their defeat, Ghanaians succeeded once again in exercising control over their own destiny. But such a recapture of their independence did not necessarily mean a return to the old order. On the contrary, like the Berbers of the Atlantic area, they too began to fight each other, and soon their once great empire degenerated into a number of petty states, each vying for power and being very jealous of the other.[42]

The end of the Almoravids' dynasty and the collapse of Ghana did not necessarily mean that Islamization ceased with the death of the Almoravid movement. The process of propagation continued and Islam began to penetrate more and more into the western Sudan. This phase in the propagation of Islam in Africa was made possible by the active involvement of three different groups of Arabo-Berber and Sudani Muslim cultivators of Islam in the West Sudan. These three groups, according to J. R. Willis and his fellow contributors in the volume entitled *Studies in West African Islamic History* (1979), are the Zawaya clerisy, the Mande Islamic clerisy, and the Torodbe clerisy. The first group has been traced to a community of Berbers who suffered oppression at the hands of fellow Berbers and Arabs. According to Willis in his comprehensive introduction to the volume cited above, the Zawaya formation began to take shape in the eleventh and twelfth centuries. They decided to be pacifists and so laid down their arms and took up the life of Muslim scholars dedicated to the propagation of Islam in the area.[47]

The Mande-Islamic clerisy emerged from the numerous trading centers created by Mande Muslims throughout the West Sudan. Because of their range of activities and the very wide area in which they lived, these men of commerce and Muslim learning came to be known by different names. They were known as Marka to the Bambara, Dafin to the peoples in the Upper Black Volta area, Yarse to the Mole-Dagbane speaking peoples, and Wangara and Djula to many others in the West Sudan. In the Senegambia area, the Jahanke (a Mande-speaking people of Serahule origins) are well-known for their historical role of peaceful promotion of Islamic culture and learning. Perhaps the best work on the Jahanke is that which was recently completed by the Gambian historian Dr. Lamin O. Sanneh. According to him, the Islamic religion was promoted by the descendants of al-Hajj Salim Suware, (the father of the Jahanke) not by the sword or through trade as is commonly thought by many scholars on the West Sudan, but through their dedication to the life of piety and scholarship.[48]

The Torodbe clerisy has been traced to manumitted slaves in Futa Toro. According to Willis and many others, the Torodbe evolved out of a mass of rootless peoples who saw in the religion of Islam an opportunity to change their subservient lives for better ones, based on Islamic solidarity and brotherhood. Those who hold this view regarding the origin of the Torodbe clerisy usually see the group only as culturally Fulbe, and so deny its members any direct and respectable connection with the ruling Fulbe classes. Such negative definitions of the Torodbe are not very correct, for it should be noted that the Islamization process also included some members of the noblemen. The detractors of the Torodbe would cite all the negative accounts in folklore mentioned by Willis in his introduction, but as he himself pointed out, among the people of Futa Toro the term Torodbe "came to be associated with the inhabitants of the villages and towns" who were committed to

Islamic learning, spoke Fulfulde and disavowed the inferior occupations.

In addition to what is said above regarding the roles of the Arabo-Berber and Sudani merchants whose activities in the West Sudan gradually led to the conversion of many African rulers and their entourages, one can also point out that Islam penetrated the southern reaches of the West Sudan through the labors of Sufi Shaykhs and divines.

Writing in January, 1977, the Gambian Islamic scholar Dr. Omar Jah of Bayero College in Kano, Nigeria, suggested that the spread of Islam in the West Sudan was to some degree accelerated by the decline and fall of Mali and Songhay. In his view, the political disintegration of these two centers "added more learned people to the group of itinerant scholars - who contributed tremendously to the dissemination of Islamic culture in the area. This situation coincided with the introduction of the Qadiri Sufi order into West Africa, under the leadership of celebrated people like the Kunti family."[49] Dr. Jah further informed that members of this order "played a prominent role in disseminating Islam in the West Sudan."[50] This view is shared by Dr. Batran, whose chapter in J. R. Willis' volume, *Studies in West African Islamic History,* is one of the best studies on the role of a leading Muslim family in the propagation of Islam in the West Sudan. Dr. Batran has recently revealed to the scholarly community that the Kunta *shaykhs* helped extend the frontiers of Islam through their longstanding custom of *Siyaha* - their peripatetic travels in pursuit of knowledge and the propagation of Islam. According to him, Sidi Ahmad Al-Bakkai was the prime mover behind the earliest dissemination of the Qadiri *wird** in the West Sudan. The family exercised great influence over the members of their Sufi order because they were noted for their learning, piety and noble pedigree.

In fact, so conscious of their origin were the members of the Kunta family that they hardly let an outsider marry one of their female members. Yet, in all their travels in the West Sudan, they did not hesitate to marry Sudani women in the various communities they settled or passed through.[51] Jenkins, who also contributed a chapter in the above-mentioned volume, has pointed out that the spread of Islam in the West Sudan could also be traced to the trade and commercial

---

*Wird is one of the rituals of an initiated member of a Sufi brotherhood. It usually consists of reciting the prayers and divine names strongly recommended by the founder of an order.

activities of the *turuq* (Sufi brotherhoods). He informs that the tendency
of the Maghribian turuq to diffuse southwards into the West Sudanic
zone culminated in their occupation of strategic position along the
trans-Saharan trade routes.

Such advantages, Jenkins argues, were enjoyed by the shaykhs
because their influence enabled them to guarantee the smooth operation
of trade and commerce along the routes under their control. This
capability to keep the peace and to protect the merchants' person and
wares (through the provision of guides to travellers and places of
lodging and board for voyagers) gave lucrative income to the leaders of
the turuq.[52] In fact, Norris, another contributor in the above-mentioned
volume, has informed us in another work of his that the Kunta controlled the salt "mine" at Ijjil (near Shinqit) in Maruetania, and that the
people paid them a paltry sum in relation to that which they received
from their customers.[53]

In order for us to understand the role of the two major Sudani clerical
groups mentioned above, we must go back to the early history of Islam in
Tekrur and Ancient Ghana. The conversion of the Tukulor (Torodbe)
and the Serahuli (Soninke)* led to their gradual emergence as active
cultivators of the faith of Islam in the West Sudan. The arrival of Islam
on the banks of the Sengal dates back a thousand years or more. The
Arabic sources tell us that Tekrur was the first Sudani Kingdom to enter
the commonwealth of Allah in the West (Maghrib) and that Ibn Yasin,
the founder of the Amoravid movement, contemplated going to Tekrur
to seek support from his Muslim co-religionists, who were then at the
helm of things in this West Sudanic society. From the same medieval and
post-medieval writers we learned that the Ghanaian kings and ruling
emperors allowed Arabo-Berber merchants to settle in their land and
that these traders from North Africa lived in their own residential areas
which served as the pivot of trade and commercial transactions between
the Muslim guests and the traditional African hosts.

As a result of these transactions, traditional Africans began to
observe Islam at work. Some of these early hosts of the Muslims, we can

---

*Here I use Serahuli because of the ambiguity associated with the term. In my part of
Africa, the term is used to describe a pagan Mandinka. I am using the term Tukulor
because the reading public is more familiar with it than with the term Torodbe. Added to
this is the fact that the term Tukulor is generally but mistakenly associated with Futa Toro
and the people therefrom.

argue, were most probably very much impressed by the religious devotion of the merchants who most likely stopped their business transactions to engage in the prescribed five daily prayers. Another area where the early Muslims could have affected the minds and hearts of the traditional Africans was their possession of the powers of the written word. This technology of intellectual conservation must have deeply impressed their early African hosts in the West Sudan, for it must have looked like a miracle to them that a man could reduce long court proceedings into signs and symbols.

In the course of this transaction flow between the North and the Sahel and the West Sudan areas, a new class of black African traders came to being. At first this body of men was very insignificant and their activity was limited to the securing of gold, slaves, and other marketable items in the North-South Saharan trade. However, as they gained knowledge of the various trade routes and cemented their relationships into religious solidarity bonds, many of these early Serahuli traders adopted the role of trader-cum-marabout. It is, indeed, against this background that one can speculate about the role of the Serahuli or any other Muslim group that entered the West Sudanic trade and helped promote the cause of Islam among their pagan African clientele.

The Serahuli contribution to the spread of Islam was not significant in the beginning. There were many reasons for this slow speed in Islamic proselytization. First of all, one can argue that Serahuli propagators of Islam were not only limited in numbers but also in effectiveness. This early phase of the Serahuli effort to propagate Islam was limited because their empire was, in the main, based on traditional African religious symbols. Things began to change when the number of Muslims increased in the West Sudan. This trend became more evident when the Ghanaian empire was about to come to an end. During this period the rulers accepted Islam and tolerated Muslim minorities trading or living within the empire by letting them occupy a certain part of the town or village.[54]

The Serahuli propagators of Islam must have constituted a part of this gradually expanding Islamic base within the West Sudan, and their activities as Marabout-cum-merchants must have prepared the ground for later expansion of their faith, even though they made no effort at direct proselytization. Indeed, it should be added that the Serahulis' activities as marabouts and traders took them to many parts of the West Sudan.

When the Mali empire replaced the Ghana empire the Serahulis, who are the northern branch of the Mande-speaking people, found themselves dispersed and weakened. Those who had converted to Islam found trading and religious instruction useful occupations. This became very clear to them when the Mali empire was firmly in the hands of Muslims. There are many historical accounts of how, under the Mali empire and the other kingdoms after it, the Marabout-cum-traders were guaranteed the right of passage at both peacetime and war.[55] The Serahulis were certainly among these traders, and Mungo Park revealed a great deal of the Serahuli preoccupation with, and love for, the west Sudanic trade, when he wrote that among the Serahuli a merchant who returns from a long trip without any exciting report of profit and gain becomes the laughingstock of his peers. Such a man, according to Mungo Park, is socially and disrespectfully described as the one who came back without anything but the hairs on his head.[56]

The Tukulors, too, have left an indelible mark on the pages of West Sudanic history. This ethnic group has given to Africa not only pastoralists, but also warriors and scholars. From their original homeland in the upper Senegal region called Futa Toro, the Tukulors have successfully migrated to different parts of the Senegambia and beyond. Indeed, it was their migration which led to the gradual expansion of Islam in the West Sudan. The activities of Fulah shepherds along the route in the West Sudan gradually opened the doors of opportunities to the inhabitants of Futa Toro. This became most evident in the late seventeenth and early eighteenth centuries, when the Tukulors and their maraboutic leaders led the Islamic revivalist movement in West Sudan. Their propagandistic drive did not only bring them into conflicts with the defenders of the African *status quo* at the time, but it also helped them conquer a huge portion of the West Sudan. These revivalist movements were a reaction to the corrupt and compromised nature of Islam in the West Sudan. With the collapse of the major West Sudanic empires, African Muslims found themselves at the mercy of traditionalists who were desperately trying to re-establish the *Ancien Regime*. Unwilling to turn the historical and religious clock backwards, and determined to concretize their longstanding dream of an Islamic state and society, some of the leading West Sudanic intellectuals saw the *Jihad* as the only solution to the problem of pagan intransigence. Another fact which must have affected their thinking and their attitude towards the traditional rulers was their knowledge of what was going on in the other parts of *Darul Islam* (the Land of Islam). B. G. Martin has written that "in West Africa, the Torodbe (Tukulor) intellectuals were not isolated from political or cultural developments in other parts of the Islamic world." He adds that Usman Dan Fodio's teacher, the Tuareg Jibril bin 'Umar al Aqdasi who had made pilgrimage to Mecca twice and was sojourned in Egypt for many years, must have passed on to the young Shehu news about the Muslim lands to the east and the determination of the dedicated ulema who wanted to wage a Jihad against the vile ulema and their traditionalist patrons.[57]

Though we may never know the exact details and the extent to which the developments in the Muslim east affected the trains of events in the West Sudan, we can say with some degree of confidence that almost all scholars agree that the revivalist idea was first put into action in Futa Jallon where the Torodbe (Tukulor) and other Fulfulbe-speaking elements ganged up on the tyrannical rulers in the name of Islamic reform.

This successful Islamic movement was led and directed by Karamoh Alfa (1726), whose victory resulted in the establishment of an *al-mamiyyah* (an Islamic order headed by an Imam) in Futa Jallon. Following the Muslim success in Futa Jallon, the idea spread to Futa Toro, where another revivalist movement, under the leadership of Sulayman Bal and Abdal Qadir, quickly took root and the traditional pagan hierarchy dismantled.[58]

After the idea of an Islamic reform had gained ground in the Senegambia region of the West Sudan, other enthusiastic reformists to the east found it useful in their own communities. The acceptance of these ideas from the two Futas gave rise to the revivalist movements of Usman Dan Fodio in Hausaland in 1804 and Shaykh Ahmad Lobbo in Macine in 1818. After this long trip to the east the idea of the jihad once again, like the Hegelian spirit, started to take a westerly course, giving rise to the jihad wars of Alhaji Omar al-Futi in Futa Toro, Bambara country and in other neighboring lands, to the revivalist efforts of Maba Jahu of the Senegambia, Samori of Mande country in Upper Guinea, Muhammadu Lamin and several other minor Jihad leaders throughout the West Sudan.[59]

The most widely celebrated hero of this age of Tukulor conquest in the name of Islam was Alhaji Omar Tall (commonly called Shaykh

Omar Futiu). This Islamic Marabout conquered much of his homeland and regions to the east. In fact, up to the time of his death he held under his rule one of the largest empires in West Africa. Unfortunately for the Shaykh, the empire he struggled hard to build fell to pieces as a result of succession feuds between his children and talibs (students). This was not new in the West Sudan, for one of the most difficult problems of rulers of empires in this part of the world has always been setting guidelines for orderly succession.

The conquest of Alhaji Omar and others like him in the West Sudan led not only to the spread of the Islamic doctrine but also to the breaking up of the traditional order in the area. The successes of Muslims in many areas of the West Sudan led to the gradual destruction of traditional cults and the emasculation of the old aristocracy.

These two processes of de-traditionalization and Islamization were going on at the same time that the West was beginning to seize African territories for the expansion of capitalism. This fact is very crucial to an understanding of the European role in the mediation between African thought and the Abrahamic tradition. That Europe came on the scene just when an embattled Africanized Islam was in the process of settling scores with an older African tradition whose foundations had been undermined over the centuries by the followers of a Holy book and a literate tradition, means a great deal to us today. Those who are interested in the big "ifs" of history can spend hours debating what would have happened had Europe's expansion into other areas of the world been delayed for a century or more; but for me, one thing is clear: that is, Africa was destined to face up to the Abrahamic challenge in another guise, and her children had to assimilate the new message from Europe and then mobilize themselves for a collective defense of their pride and dignity. Whereas in the earlier days Africans fought and traded with Arab bearers of one version of the Abrahamic heritage, under European rule Africa's peoples became the reluctant subjects of a western civilization in search of converts. It is this tragic experience with the western civilization that I wish to unravel in the next chapter. My purpose is not necessarily to pour fuel into the fires of racial conflicts resulting from the European blunder in Africa, but to trace in brief outline the western conquest of Africa and the resultant planting of Christianity. But before proceeding to the next chapter let us trace the history of Islam in Eastern and Central Africa.

After discussing the rise and spread of Islam in the West Sudan, let us now look at its penetration of the Eastern Sudan. By the term Eastern Sudan, I mean that geographical area which is now called the Republic of Sudan. The religion of Muhammad came to the Eastern Sudan because certain factors propelled the Arab conquerors of Coptic Egypt to move southwards into the regions below the Aswan. One of the major factors was the harassment of Arab Muslim settlements by the Nubians and Bejas. The former were not very happy with the Arabs whose conquest of Egypt brought their Christian co-religionists under Arab domination. Another factor which led to the Arab attempt to conquer and rule the Eastern Sudan was the trade and commercial interest of their mercantile classes. A third would be the desire of the religiously-devout to gain a foothold for Islam in Nubi and Beja countries.

According to the Sudanese scholar Yusuf Fadl Hassan, the Arab Muslims were able to enter the area by three routes. The first was across the Red Sea, either through Ethiopian territory or directly to the Red Sea ports of Badi, Aydhab and Suakin. In Hassan's view, the number of immigrants who took the Red Sea route must have been significant when compared to the large numbers who inched their way through Misr (Egypt). This second route was largely responsible for the gradual but successful Arabization and Islamization of the Eastern Sudan. Many Arab immigrants wangled their way into Nubian territory without the permission of the authorities. The last route, according to Fadl Hassan, was the least significant: the North-West African route through which many religious men passed. This was the path of the Sufi men of Islam who travelled from the West Sudan to Mecca or Egypt, or who took and promoted their religious causes from the North African desert to the land of the Baja and of the other groups located along the Nile valley. The relationship between the Muslims and the Christian Nubians remained peaceful on account of the strict observance by both parties of the Baqt treaty, which remained the foundation of Muslim-Nubian relations for over six centuries. Though the terms of the Baqt treaty specifically stated that a citizen of one of the two countries could not stay permanently in the other, evidence shows that Muslim traders began to enter Nubia soon after the treaty, and their growing numbers were to serve as the basis for an eventual takeover by Islamic forces.[60]

According to Fadl Hassan, "the end of Christian Nubia came at the

hands of the Muslim Arabs, who had for centuries entered in small
numbers from Upper Egypt."[61] He adds that Al-Maris was the first
region to feel the impact, because here the Arab elements settled and
intermarried with the local inhabitants. This arrangement proved quite
favorable to the expansion of Islam. One factor which has always
worked in favor of the Arabs in the whole region called Bilad Al-Sudan
was the matrilineal system of which the Arabs took full advantage, and
so landed themselves in positions of chiefly power in their newly
adopted homes. The Banu a'l-Kanz were the main beneficiaries of the
Nubian matrilineal system, and in a very short time, they became the
virtual rulers of the region of Al-Maris.

This process of settlement and penetration of Nubian lands by the
Arabs continued and in time the Muslims seized control of the Nubian
throne. This came when Sayf al-Din 'Abdullah Barshambu, the nephew
of King Dawud, was made King by the Mamluk forces. He was the
third puppet king appointed by the Mamluk but he was the first to
profess Islam. With his conversion the door was opened for the massive
Islamization of the entire Kingdom.[62] With the Nubians gradually
drawn into Darul Islam, the Arabs began to fish for more converts
elsewhere.

The relationship between the Arabs and the peoples of the western
coast of the Red Sea dates back to the lifetime of the Prophet. At the
height of the Meccan persecution, he advised some of his followers to
migrate to Abyssinia. This major incident in early Islamic history made
these peoples no strangers to the Muslims. As early as 640 A.D., the
Muslim merchants were already active in the area; in fact, a Muslim
migrated to Badi (one of the Sudanese ports) in the same year. Through
trade and warfare the Muslims gradually penetrated and conquered the
Beja territory.

At first the Beja were nominal Muslims, but after many attacks and
counter-attacks, the spirit of Islam gradually conquered the Beja and
Muslims became the predominant force in the area. Mosques came into
being, trade and commerce flourished, and so the Beja became part of
the wider world of Islam. Soon the voice of the Muezzin was heard
from Aswan to Massawa. This gradual Arabization and Islamization of
Beja country intensified during the reign of Al-Mu'tasim, whose Turki-
fication program deprived many Arab Muslims of their pension rights.
This act of the new ruler of Egypt drove many of the Arabs to farming,

and many opted to settle permanently in Beja country. This mass settlement of Arabs in Beja country and the Eastern Sudan, plus the fact that between 1058 and 1261 pilgrims from Egypt and North-West Africa passed through Beja country on their way to Mecca, exposed the Beja more and more to the influences of Islam.

Although Islam has not succeeded in winning the hearts of all the inhabitants of the Eastern Sudan, we can conclude this brief survey by saying that, in the Islamization of the peoples of the Eastern Sudan, conflict of interest between invading Arabs and self-protecting Eastern Sudanis, trade and religious instruction were the means by which the children of Darul Islam brought the area under their control. As Fadl Hassan concludes in his paper in the volume edited by I. W. Lewis, "the process of Islamization was accompanied by a process of Arabization which left its mark on a large part of the country; for Arabic was not only the language of Islam but also of trade."[63]

When we move farther south to what is today called the Horn of Africa, we find that the arrival of Islam in Somalia and Ethiopia dates back to the early period of Islam. In fact, long before the birth of Prophet Muhammad, many transactions were conducted across the Red Sea. Though the sea had been taken as a very difficult one to navigate, it was never looked at as a formidable obstacle to the Arabs and the peoples of the Horn. The beginning of Islam goes back to the attempts of Arab merchants of the rising Islamic state to gain a foothold in the area and to expand their trade opportunities. As in the other areas of the world where the Arabs came into contact with new peoples, here too, the usual patterns of trade, commerce and intermarriage developed.

In his study of Islam in the Horn of Africa, Trimingham sees two strains of Islamic culture. There is on the one hand that of the nomads, and on the other that of the sedentary village or town dwellers. In the first case, Trimingham asserts, Islam exercises practically no influence in the life of the pagans. Where Islam is accepted, however, three stages become evident. In the first stage, there is superficial adoption of Islamic ways, and this is reflected in the borrowing of certain material elements associated with the Islamic culture. In the second stage, actual elements of Islamic religious culture are adopted and assimilated. The third stage, which is very revolutionary in its effects, consists of transforming the person into a Muslim who is genuinely convinced of the efficacy of Islamic sanctions and hence, is willing to change his customs and habit of conduct.[64]

If we are to accept this model of Islamization worked out by Tri-mingham, we can conclude by saying that among the numerous Muslim peoples in the Horn there are many persons who fall under one of his three stages of Islamic development. But since Trimingham's model is meant for the scholars who are interested in working out the finer points in the psychological and psycho-cultural manifestations of human encounters with new forces within his social universe, we can briefly say in passing that Islam has succeeded in gaining a firm foothold in Somalia where, I. W. Lewis tells us, Islamic orthodoxy under the leadership of two Sufi Turuq (Qadiriyya and Ahmadiyya) seems to be faring well. Besides the Somalis, there are the Galla and the Harari peoples of Ethiopia who have joined the fold of Islam.[65]

Islamization is very weak in some parts of this region, and the people who lend empirical support to Trimingham's theoretical model of Islamic assimilation are the Borans. According to P. T. W. Baxter, this African ethnic group, whose members are found between the Republic of Somalia and Kenya, has yet to be fully Islamic. The main influence of Islam is evident only in the realm of material culture. The valuational and institutional bases of Islamic culture have yet to take root. Baxter further informs that only those Borans who have been drawn within the cultural net of the Muslim Somalis are Islamized and, hence, assimilated to the Somali view of Islam.[66]

The arrival of Islam in East and Central Africa goes back to the settlement of the East African coast by the Shirazi and the Arabs. The evidence that is now available to the historians of East Africa suggests that very few of the merchants from the East settled in the area at the early phase of their contact with the coast. Gradually, however, things changed. These changes were largely exogenously inspired. In fact, it was due to political developments in Arabia and Persia that some elements from the East began to settle in towns along the East African coast. According to Neville Chittick, the Shirazi immigrants first moved to the Somali coast and then resettled themselves along the coastal towns of East Africa. By the time many of these Shirazi immi-grants came to the Shungwaya region, most of them were racially mixed with the Bantu peoples of the area. As a result of these intermar-riages, one can assume Islam began to gain a few converts here and there among the Bantus. Yet, in making this assumption, one must bear in mind that these settlements were destined to have very limited contact with the hinterland. Even when the Arabs came over to the coast from Hadhramaut, Oman and other points in the Persian Gulf, things did not change. Much of what we learn from the chronicles of such major towns as Lamu, Mombasa, Kilwa, Pate and Malindi, relates to the rivalries and feuds between the ruling classes of these coastal settlements.[67]

The coastal towns began to influence the life and history of the peoples of the interior only after 1800. Prior to this time, we do not know how and where the coastal towns got the goods which they put out on the Indian Ocean market. What has been suggested was that the gold from south-central Africa nourished much of the coast in the days before the arrival of the Portuguese. According to F. J. Berg, at this time in East African Coastal history, "most of the towns do not seem to have enjoyed a flourishing commerce. Ordinary citizens appear often to have lived by cultivating *Shamba* near their city, frequently on the mainland if the town were on an island."[68] As a result of this new arrangement, settlements on Pemba and the Kenya coast traded extensively in grain with southern Arabia. This was the most important international commercial activity at the coast.[69] Indirect trade with the interior supplemented agriculture and grain shipping. The middlemen in this new trade were the Nyika and the "Mozungullo." These peoples served as go-betweens, and soon a new era in the history of the East African region began.

As Norman R. Bennett pointed out in his chapter on the Arab impact in East Africa, in the volume on East African History published by the Historical Association of Kenya, the initial stimulus for this new relationship between the coastal peoples and the hinterland came from the Africans from the interior. The most prominent of these interior peoples were the Nyawezi, Yao, Bisa and the Kamba. These groups opened the routes to the Arabs who were keen about gaining footholds in the inland areas. This new connection soon enabled the Arabs to penetrate further and further into East and Central Africa. Bennett identified three major routes which these coastal Arab and Swahili peoples used to get access into the lands of ivory, gold and slaves.[70] As I pointed out in the section dealing with the Beja, the Arabs in most cases capitalized on the matrilineal and social systems of the Africans. By contracting marriages with their African hosts they soon endeared themselves to some of the ruling families in the area. As a result of such marriages they benefitted from the loyalties and material support of their in-laws.

The Arab penetration of East and Central Africa was, however, not an easy one. There were many instances when their presence was resented and resisted by the Africans. But as is stated by many observers and historians, the Africans suffered at the hands of these ruthless Arab and Swahili traders largely because they failed to unite and act as a collective force in face of Arab aggression. Yet, in stating this fact, it should also be noted that there were many cases where Africans aligned themselves with the Arabs out of self-interest. This became the case in instances where the African ruler found himself the target of fierce rivalry and jealousy from many African quarters.

In assessing the progress of Islam in East and Central Africa, one must bear in mind that the religion of Islam was not vigorously promoted by the Arab traders. These men were very business-oriented and, hence, cared very little about the stocks of Islam in the area. In fact, Bennett tells us that with the exception of Buganda, Islam made no significant progress in the region. The peoples who embraced Islam were mainly those who were partners in plunder and trade with the Arabs from the coast.[71] The Yao and the Nyawezi were among the most active partners of the coastal traders and any list of East or Central African ethnic groups that have joined the fold of Islam must include their names.

In Southern Africa, the Arabs were never a significant factor, and hence, one cannot identify South African Islam with them. The promoters of Islam in the Republic of South Africa were the Malaysian and Indian coolies who were brought into that part of Africa by the Europeans. These groups of non-whites are active Muslims, and they are well-known in international Islamic circles. If one is to make a judgement, then it should be stated that Islam has a great prospect in South Africa once the fetters of apartheid are thrown away and the non-white majority assumes the reins of government in a multi-racial society based on majority rule. This point is made on the grounds that the long oppression of the non-white population in the Republic of South Africa has a negative effect on the minds of the educated elements of the discriminated majority. This will be more so with the young Africans who are born Christian and have earned belatedly that the racists in their country have appropriated the Bible to legitimize their racial rule. Such young people are likely to be bitter with the system and the Christian churches and they are often more receptive to radical materialist ideologies.

On the social plane, the conversion of the tribal African to the religion of Muhammad opened, to a certain degree, the door of inter-ethnic cooperation. The fact that the Muslim propagators were, in most cases, merchants, made the converts more receptive to the new ideas and new wares brought into their areas by their fellow co-religionists. What I am suggesting here is that, even if there were trade ties between a non-Muslim people and traders of Muslim background, the fact that they willingly entered such relationships exposed them to Islamic mode of trade and commerce, for as McCall points out, Islam provided a common moral basis for commerce and trade and the Sharia guided all the Muslim merchants in their dealings with one another and with their non-Muslim customers. According to him, Islam "may have been advantageous to Sudanese merchants in . . . another way. In areas of endemic conflict there is a need for a neutral to serve as go-between. He must be easily recognized so that he would not be attacked by either side by mistake."[72] Working on this assumption, McCall further asserts that the Muslim clothing in the eleventh century West Sudan was probably as effective as tatooing in nineteenth century Typee or calabashes in the sixteenth century Mississippi Valley. In all these above mentioned cases, the parties to conflicts granted special treatment to those who, by virtue of their trade or profession, were considered non-combatants.[73]

The close relationship between trade and Islam made it possible for the new convert to develop gradually some degree of trust and confidence in men who do not necessarily speak his language but who embrace the teachings of his newly adopted religion. This new attitude towards non-members of one's ethnic group is certainly revolutionary, and its potential for greater inter-ethnic cooperation could not be dismissed lightly. Though Islam was not the factor responsible for the immediate founding of the three great West Sudanese empires, the fact remains that these empires and their rulers profited from the Islamic symbols of their day and their cultural and economic systems were, in varying degrees, exposed to the forces and pressures of the faraway Islamic centers of civilization to the north and northeast.

In fact, in talking about the Islamic contribution to the social universe of the African, one could argue that the arrival of Islam in the continent widened the horizons of the traditional African a little bit. Whereas in the past this man had entrusted destiny to the hands of the spirits who resided in a well, a tree or a stream somewhere in the ecological setting

of his tribal group, whereas he wished to placate the gods and the
ancestors, under the Islamic religion he found that his life was for an
appointed time and that his deeds on earth did have singular meaning.
He also learned from his Islamic mentors that whatever he did in his
lifetime would be accounted for in the hereafter, and the only way he
could save his soul and himself at the Day of Judgement was to accept
the responsibility of living. This is to say that the conversion of the
traditional African meant his gradual realization of the spiritual loneli-
ness of man in the world and his responsibility to live up to the
expectations of his religion. Such an understanding of self and life gave
rise to the attempt on the part of many African converts to put into
effective practice (or sloppy practice) the rituals and teachings of Islam.

It is indeed in their attempt to live up to the Islamic ideal that many
traditional Africans learn to pray with fellow Muslims, or to stand alone
before Allah. In their desire to win the favors of their Maker, they now
learn to fulfill the expectations of the Quranic teachings on cleanliness
and modesty in clothing. Writing on what the religion of Islam implied
to the African convert some years before the European powers successfully partitioned the greater part of the African continent, R. Bosworth
Smith, in his *Mohammedanism in Africa* (1887), identified many areas in the
African social universe where Islam was beginning to establish itself and
its influence. He noted that the adoption of Islam by traditional Africans
raised their sense and understanding of hygiene and that it made them
more and more aware of the Islamic belief that the covering of one's
physical nakedness is a great step towards the covering of one's spiritual
nakedness before Allah. Smith also pointed out that the arrival of Islam
in the West Sudan broadened the basis of social solidarity and, in the
language of Ibn Khaldun, gave rise to a new Assabiyya (social solidarity) of some sort, which in turn led to the formation of supertribal or
imperial political organizations. This process of growing political consciousness among the Muslims of diverse ethnic backgrounds, in Smith's
view, was largely due to the community of sentiments created by Islam.
He also believed that the religion of Islam had a great impact on
traditional African society because it ushered in a revolution in the
mental estate of the individual. He sums his view of the Islamic impact
this way:

> As regards the individual, it is admitted on all hands that Islam gives to its
> new Negro converts an energy, a dignity, a self-reliance, and a self-

respect which is all too rarely found in their Pagan or their Christian
fellow countrymen.[74]

On the cultural plane, we can also argue that the advent of Islam
meant a great deal for many African societies. If we identify the
material, value and institutional bases of a society as the essential aspects
of its culture, then we can proceed to demonstrate the manner in which
the religion of Muhammad affected the cultural realm of traditional
African man. First of all we can say that the advent of the religion of
Islam in the West Sudanese states of the medieval period led to the
penetration of Arab and Berber merchants. The trade and commercial
ties between the states in the Maghrib and their sisters to the East, on the
one hand, and the Black African Kingdoms to the south of the Sahara
Desert on the other, led to the slave raids and slave trade across the
Sahara. This did not only deplete the kingdoms in the forest belts of
thousands of human beings who were forced to leave their homes and
never to return, but it also laid the foundation for Arab and Berber
invasion of Ghana in 1076. Indeed, one can argue that the trade and
commerce between the Arabo-Berber states to the North and the
sub-Saharan states was one of the reasons for the depopulation of
African kingdoms below the Sahel. There is also evidence that the
colonization of the continent by Europeans was partly motivated by
their desire to wrest power and trade routes from their Muslim rivals in
the Mediterranean. Within this context, one can further maintain that
Africa's woes and wounds were the products of the Arabo-Berber quest
for gold and slaves. Such physical and psychological injuries could also
be attributed to the treachery of some of sub-Saharan Africa's own
children whose greed and ruthlessness revealed the baser instincts of the
overpowerful human being.

Islam, it can be argued, was not really the motivating force behind
such atrocities. Like Christianity in later years, it, too, was an instrument of rationalization. When viewed from this perspective, we can
then suggest that Europe's "discovery" and subsequent colonization of
Africa were the result of the frantic efforts of Europeans who wished to
weaken Islamic power in the name of Christianity and to establish
imperial preserves in glorification of their newly fashioned national-
isms. Though some aggressive European nationalists might have seen
Christianity as a horse that could transport them to the "Dark Continent," where they could play out their self-appointed role as cosmic

transformers, the fact remains that this Christian horse was very much reluctant to follow the riders' commands. Yet, in saying this, we must concede the fact that this religious horse was in most cases treated by the colonial power as a Trojan horse from Europe to Africa. As a result of these nationalistic and political usages of the religion, Christianity came to be seen by many Africans as a tool in the service of Caesar, a point which was very much resented by devout Christians from the metropole.

At the institutional level, one can argue that the religion of Islam introduced several changes in African life. The arrival of a Muslim scholar into an African community most often led to the establishment of the Madrasseh (Quranic schools). This new institution gradually replaced, or co-existed with, the traditional centers of education, and the students who were brought before the Quranic teacher were slowly inducted into the Islamic culture from the north and northeast.

Besides the Quranic school, there were other institutional forms of cultural borrowing. With the gradual penetration of the African con- sciousness, Islam began to invade the African conceptual world and soon the process of linguistic imbibition started to take effect. Con- sciously or unconsciously, the newly converted African Muslim began to drop traditional words in his language in favor of borrowed Islamic terminology. A classic example of an African language that has been very much penetrated by the Arabo-Islamic influence is Wolof. The arrival of Islam did not only affect the Wolof's conception of time, but it also replaced many Arabic terms in his vocabulary. As an illustration, let us take the names given to the seven days of the week. As a result of the Arabo-Islamic influence, the Wolof language as spoken in the Senegambian region carries four Arabic words for Tuesday (Arabic Thalatah), Wednesday (Al-Arba), Thursday (Al-khamsah) and Friday (Al-Jummah). This is a phenomenon that is widely known in the African communities which have established long contact with the Islamic religion. Commenting on this aspect of the African-Islamic encounter, I. W. Lewis put it this way:

> The Muslim lunar calendar is everywhere adopted with Islam, and tends to displace other systems of time-reckoning, except where these are very firmly embedded in an unchanging seasonal cycle of economic interests. . . . Generally, however, the Arabic names for the Muslim months are adopted, although alternate local names based on an earlier calendar may also be utilized, as well as direct vernacular translations expressive of the religious and social content of the month in question.[75]

Another example of institutional borrowing was the *Tariqa* (Sufi brotherhood). As Nehemia Levtzion correctly points out, these bodies became significant in the West Sudan only in the eighteenth and nineteenth centuries.[76] But in noting this point we should bear in mind that the arrival of the Sufi brotherhoods ushered in a train of development which affected the history of many African societies south of the Sahara. It is well-known in the growing literature on the Islamic jihads in Africa south of the Sahara that the followers of the Sufi brotherhoods played an important role. It was men like Usman Dan Fodio, Alhaji Omar, Maba Jahu, Sait Mati, Foday Kaba, Shaikh Muhammad Abdille Hassan, The Mahdi Muhammad Ahmad ibn Abdallah and several other minor historical figures in the West Sudan, who carried the Islamic banner against those whom almost all of them perceived as unbelievers. Some of these jihad warriors felt that it was their duty to purge Islam of decadence and corruption and, for this reason, some of them were quite willing to wage war against those whom they perceived as vile ulema.[77] In light of these developments, one could argue that the successful adaptation of the Sufi brotherhood in the West Sudan contributed to the growth of Muslim solidarity and cohesiveness at the elite level. In fact, I am inclined to believe that the growing acculturation of African Muslims in the Islamic culture together with their desire to play a more active role in the political systems of their times might have led many of them to agitate for reform and change in the lives of their non-Muslim peoples.

The last contribution of Islam to be discussed in this section is the successful adoption of the Arabic script for the reduction of African languages into writing. This Arabo-Islamic cultural contribution is by no means insignificant. Indeed such a development in Africa's cultural history led to the emergence of a limited form of literacy among many of the Muslim peoples of the West Sudan. The first products of this newly imported technology of intellectual conservation were the epistles and explanatory comments written down by the ulema in the West Sudan. It is quite conceivable that many of the West Sudanic ulema found it desirable from time to time to reduce to writing their thoughts on certain matters affecting the education of their students. Another possible reason for the emergence of the written forms of the vernacular was the desire of the more aggressive propagators of the religion to make their message more accessible to the rank and file of their Islamic movement.[78]

Writing on the development of the vernacular languages in West African zones of Islam and Christianity, some scholars have recently suggested that the earlier literary products of the African vernacular languages that adopted Arabic or even a European language, cannot be classified as literature. They were merely the first manifestation of a foreign script at the service of an African language. They also believe, and quite correctly, that "... such texts in the West African languages were usually merely parallel to the more important and prestigious originals in the particular languages of the given cultures and powers."[79]

But regardless of the limitations of the newly established technology of intellectual conservation, there are strong evidences that such a development had a great impact on the traditional African's social universe. Edward Blyden, the celebrated Black intellectual, was very much impressed by the influence of Islam on the black man. He and some of his Christian contemporaries thought that the advance of the religion of Islam was a prologue to the real drama, which would be the gradual and final Christianization of the African man. Blyden, in his attempt to demonstrate the cultural impact of Islam, quoted Barth as saying that some of the vernaculars had been enriched "by expressions from the Arabic for the embodiment of the higher processes of thought." He added that, "they have received terms regarding the religion of one God, and respecting a certain state of civilization, such as marrying, reading, writing, and the objects have relation thereto, sections of time, and phrases of salutation and of good breeding; then the term relating to dress, instruments, and the art of warfare as well as architecture, commerce ..."[80]

3

THE WESTERN CONQUEST AND AFRICAN SOCIETY

*T*he European conquest of Africa has resulted in the most radical transformation of African society by foreign invaders. Not only has the African landscape been altered drastically by the machines issuing from the scientifically inspired and technologically created factories of European man, but his very mental world has come under the direct influence of western civilization. One of the most important areas of African mental life which is now very much affected by Western Civilization is his world view. This part of African life is now dominated by the Abrahamic tradition. Whether the African intellectual likes it or not his mental world is yet to be exorcised from the ghosts of Abrahamic thought. It is true that traditional African thought still holds sway among a large percentage of Africa's population, but the fact remains that the Islamic and Christian brands of the Abrahamic tradition between them have the greater number of Africans within their folds.

This success of the two forms of the Abrahamic tradition is largely due to the manner in which they entered into the African's world and mind. Islam came as a religion of Arab conquerors, merchants and marabouts; it gained a foothold as its propagators established for themselves trading depots and exchanged goods with Africans. This commerce and trade led to the flow of ideas, and gradually Islam won indigenous converts who fund in the religion the answer to their souls' yearnings. Christianity, on the other hand, gained a foothold because of its status as the conqueror's religion. Added to this, and more significantly, was the fact that European colonization brought in a train of novelties and opportunities which dazzled the eyes of many an illiterate African who reluctantly yielded to their seductive powers. To put it another way, I would say the advent of European colonialism provided the non-Islamized Africans with the unsolicited opportunity to partake in a civilization that was abroad to promote itself and to demonstrate its overall superiority with science and technology that are reduceable to writing. That the traditional African was not in the habit of employing or developing the technology of intellectual conservation in the centuries before European colonialism in Africa is well known. What, however, is not generally discussed by most people is the fact that the western conquest of African society was more mental than material; and that Christianity, though still a struggling plant in an alien African soil, played an active part in the *westernization* of African man and the *semitization* of African thought.

A.1. The Christian View of Life

The Christian view of life is deeply rooted in the biblical tradition. Yet, even though one can go back to the Old Testament to trace some of the theological roots in the Christian doctrine, the fact remains that the most important elements are derived from the teachings of the founder of the Christian faith and of his most influential peripatetic follower, St. Paul. Jesus said in the gospels that he did not come to break the laws of the House of Israel, but to fulfill them. This view was not accepted by his Jewish contemporaries, for, as the early history of the Church shows, Christ's mission was soon to be misconstrued for temporal aggrandizement by his detractors and this quickly led to his crucifixion.

Unlike the Jewish contemporaries of Christ who refused to accept him as the fulfillment of their age-old prophecies, the members of the early Christian Church saw themselves as the witnesses of the descent of God Himself in human flesh. These disciples enthusiastically accepted the claims of their Master as the Messiah sent to redeem humanity from the bondage of carnal sin. In so doing, these early Christians believed that Christ's message and mission on earth were unique and unduplicable in the realm of Being. This self-definition plus the New Testament teachings on the role and place of Christ's suffering in human history combined to give Christianity a unique place among world religions.[81] Such a belief in the Incarnation of God Himself also distinguished the Christian from the other beneficiaries of the Abrahamic tradition. Whereas the follower of Judaism would tell anyone who cares to listen that God had a covenant with the House of Israel and that the history of the children of Israel is the dialogue between the Heavenly Kingdom and the Israelites favored and chosen by God, he would never say that God Himself entered history as a human person to put an end to the old pre-Christian age of sin and shame. Whereas the Muslim neighbor of the Christian believer may tell him that the Al-Quran is the *actual word of Allah*, he would undoubtedly refrain from associating the Divine with a human figure acting as God Himself in history.

In Christian thought, the Incarnation is the most important historical event, because the very foundation of the Church depends on it. In fact, all other beliefs hinge upon this one. We cannot understand the nature, role and place of man in the cosmic scheme of things unless and until we are convinced that Christ took human form to fulfill what the Christians believe to be the prophecies of the ancient prophets of Israel. If the founder of the Christian faith did not fulfill the Hebraic prophecies about the Messiah, then there was no Savior, and if there was no Savior, then there was no crucifixion and no resurrection. In other words, to the Christian, the coming of Christ gave meaning to history. Without the incarnation of Christ, history is meaningless and life would indeed be, in the language of Shakespeare's Macbeth, a tale told by a cosmic idiot, full of sound and fury, signifying nothing.

Taking the Christian concept of Incarnation as a point of departure, we can say that almost all Christians believe life is a gift from the Creator and that man is created in the image of God. This Christian view is commonly shared with the other branches of the Abrahamic tradition. Both the Jew and the Muslim believe that man was specially created by God and life is a divine gift to the children of Adam, the first human creation of the Maker of the Universe. Although this concept has been the subject of numerous theological treatises and disputations[82], we can say with some degree of confidence that the doctrine means two things. First, it teaches that, like the rest of creation, man is dependent upon God for his coming into existence and for the maintenance of his life on earth. Secondly, that he is created with special capacities which put him very much above the rest of creation. Because of this unique position of man, God has decided to maintain a spiritual dialogue with him through the medium of prophecy. In the Christian understanding of Jewish history, the children of Israel were marked out as God's Chosen People who were bound by a Divine Covenant to act out on the stage of history the laws of the Creator.

Writing on this aspect of the history of Israel, Arend Theodoor van Leeuwen puts it this way:

> The great theme of God's historical activity in the Old Testament is that of gathering and scattering and gathering again. The whole earth was one; they were scattered (Gen. 11); but in the latter days they shall forgather again (Is. 2). This basic theme is then developed rather like a figure; that is, the theme is reiterated in the history of God's dealings

with the people of Israel. Though all mankind upon earth is scattered
abroad, its hidden unity remains preserved in the people which the Lord
brings forth out of Abram ... Israel, therefore, represents all mankind, in
unity and scattering, in pride and sin and fall. God's judgement upon all
the earth; and when the Lord has mercy on his people and gathers them
again, the action adumbrates his blessings which he has promised to
bestow on each and every nation; her history is the center and epitome of
all history and the revelation of God's purposes for all mankind.[83]

This divine purpose for the children of Israel was not fulfilled. In
Christian theology there is almost a consensus that the coming of Christ
put an end to the Old Covenant. In other words, Christ fulfilled the
prophecies of the ancient Jewish prophets and at the same time endured
the "judgement of God, entailed by the people of Israel's failure to be
the salt of the earth." In fulfilling these prophecies and in bringing into
being a New Covenant, Jesus Christ is telling the gentiles that Israel's
failures are symbolically those of humanity; and that since they have
never attempted to enter the New Jerusalem provided, they are ready
and willing to repent for their sins and to hold on tightly to the rope of
Christ, linking the New Jerusalem to the Eternal City wherein Jesus
Christ sits at the right hand of God.

One point that grows out of the Christian notion of incarnation in
that, unlike some of the Jews who believe that human beings are
incapable of satisfying the demands of integral righteousness, the followers of Christ believe with St. Paul that many of them who "were
baptized into Jesus Christ were baptized into his death" and "if (they)
have been planted together in the likeness of his death, (they) shall be
also in the likeness of his resurrection." In this epistle to the Romans, St.
Paul reminds his fellow believers that the resurrection of Christ has a
very positive eschatological meaning for the true Christian believer. He
reminds them that the body of sin of the Christian "is crucified with him
(Jesus), that the body of sin might be destroyed, that henceforth (Christians) should not serve sin. For he that is dead is freed from sin."

Paul continues his argument by saying, "Now if we be dead with
Christ, we believe that we shall also live with him ..."[84] In another letter
to the Colossians, he states:."If ye then be risen with Christ, seek those
things which are above, where Christ sitteth on the right hand of God.
Set your affection on things above, not on things on the earth. For ye are
dead, and your life is hid with Christ in God...Mortify therefore your
members which are upon the earth."[85] These teachings of St. Paul were

destined to have great ramifications for the history of Western man and for the members of Christendom. According to Erich Kahler, to whom we owe the debt for referring us to the above passages of St. Paul, these words of St. Paul set the stage for the gradual secularization of human life and history. Continuing on this note, Kahler puts it this way:

> Here is the onset of that crucial division of the physical and spiritual spheres which subsequently kept growing to the point of complete secularization of human life on earth, and so of history. In the Jewish pilgrimage to the kingdom of God, however infinitely protracted, life on earth was not separated from life in the spirit. Within earthly life and time, man, every man, was called on to contribute towards the ultimate realization of the divinized world. The deification of Christ, however, and the assumption of the vicarious passion by which he absolves all true believers — as dogmatically interpreted by Paul — generated an inescapable contradiction. On the other hand, the advent of the kingdom of God on earth, preceded by the Day of Judgement, was still expected to occur in the near future with the *Parousia* of Jesus Christ. On the other hand, the baptism of the individual believer, his having died and risen again with Christ and thereafter "living in Christ," forestalled and anticipated for that individual the effect of the Second Coming; and aiming at things which are above, and not (at) things on the earth," a life..." hid with Christ in God," and mortification of the "members which are upon the earth." Thus, a life in this world, a life in time, where the Kingdom of God has yet to come, severs with a hidden life "above," where the salvation of the individual believer is already achieved. The unique descent of God into human form guaranteed earthly realization of salvation, and this "event par excellence" consolidated history on earth. But the unsustainable tension between the above and the below, which Paul derived from it, gave rise to a development which was bound ultimately to surrender history to complete secularity.[86]

These words of Kahler may be disputed by some Christians, but there is evidence that the history of Christianity has been a movement towards secularization. This view can be based upon the record of western society, where Christian man has traveled much farther along the road to materialism. In fact, one can argue that this movement towards secularization has affected even the thinkers and writers of the church.[87]

Since the Renaissance, many Western scholars and theologians have tried to harmonize the teachings of Christ with the dominant philosophies of history of their times. Up to the time of the Renaissance, the greater majority of Christians in the West accepted the providential view of history. Voltaire is said to have been the one who gave the *coup de grace* to this old moral and theological view of history. As M.C. D'Arcy correctly points out, there were, however, other factors which contributed to the change of mind. A major one that needs to be emphasized is that the eighteenth century ended with the apotheosis of reason. European man was beginning to make inroads in the natural and physical sciences; he was also extending his dominion over the world by conquering other areas of the planet which were previously isolated from his civilizational orbit. At this point in European history, "the weather-vane was veering to man and the progress of man, and the Christian hope in the after-life was changing to a hope of secular progress. Christian values and the indirect fruits of Christian teaching did not die, but the framework of the old theology was ignored."[88] This primacy of reason affected the whole of Western Society and thought and even those thinkers who professed a form of Christian belief, like Hegel, exploited heaven and earth in terms of mind. D'Arcy captures the dominant spirit of this time when he writes:

> "Not only was the wardrum to throb no longer and the battle flag to be furled in the Parliament of Man, the Federation of the World, but man was to come 'on that which is,' and catch 'the deep pulsations of the world, Aeolian music measuring out the steps of time, the shocks of chance, the blows of death.' God, as Browning wrote, was to be the 'time confederate' and lose his mystery. The aim was to make history truly scientific and so to control events that the future would be predictable."[89]

Of course, the age of reason was soon to be overtaken by human events and the unbridled optimism of Voltaire and his successors was later succeeded by the pessimism of Schopenhauer and Nietzsche and the empiricism of Comte and Marx. With the death of Hegel, European and Western societies began to fall completely under the spell of the scientist.[90] The philosophers lost their prominent place in the intellectual world of Western man, and Christian thinkers no longer found it attractive enough to "tailgate" the intellectual caravans of those philosophers who tried very hard to continue the tradition of system-building in philosophy. In other words, with the domination of human life and thought by the scientists of Western society, the religious thinkers found it more and more fashionable to think and rethink their theories of history within the dominant scientific framework. This led to the dominance in Christian circles of ideas derived from positivism, liberalism, and historicism. Such a pattern continued until 1919, when Karl Barth championed a new orthodoxy in Western theological circles. In his monumental *Church Dogmatics* (13 volumes, 1936-69), he elaborated upon his concept of the primacy of God and he counterposed his new orthodoxy to the prevailing emphasis on immanentism, historicism, social action, and the idea of progress.[91]

In many respects Barth was reacting to the modernizing efforts of the liberal theologians. These liberal modernist thinkers in the Christian churches, were very much impressed by the works of Darwin and others after him. The findings of men like Darwin led to the gradual abandonment of the old idea of divine immanence in nature and the adoption of the idea of the indwelling of God in man. W.M. Horton, in an essay entitled, "The Development of Theological Thought," notes the trend of events in the following passage:

> "When this was carried to the extreme a religion of humanity not far removed from Auguste Comte's was the logical outcome. In Germany, the theology of Scheimecher leaned more toward the first extreme, and that of Ritschl toward the second. In France, Britain, and America, the influence of two types of theology was concurrent and about equal; so Liberalism in these countries was held in a more moderate position by these two opposite pulls.[92]

Since the publication of Barth's *Romans*, Christian thinkers have responded to his call for neo-orthodoxy in different ways. Because our intention here is not to follow the debate in detail, we trace the development of post-Barthian theological thought and see how it adds to our understanding of the modern Christian view of man and history. After a close look at the bibliographical data available to the researchers of this subject, one is inclined to state that since the appearance of Barth's pioneering study, the Western and Christian world has been caught in a great debate over three major issues. The first deals with biblical and historical criticism in its bearing on the truth of the Christian revelation; the second addresses itself to natural science (especially the doctrine of evolution) in its relation to the doctrines of creation and providence; and finally, the third deals with the social problems created by the industrial revolution and their bearing on the application of Christian ethics and the hope of the kingdom of God.[93]

These three issues have generated much interest in biblical history and the philosophy of history in the Christian world, and many devout Christian scholars have tried to reduce to writing their own reflections on the problem. Introducing a volume of essays, *God, History and Historians: An Anthology of Modern Christian Views of History* (1977), Professor C.T. McIntire tells us that the renewal of interest in Christian view of history emerges from two main sources. The primary one is a response to the catastrophies of the secular age. Its most serious manifestations were the bloodbath associated with the First and Second World Wars. In both instances man proved to be incapable of governing himself and the universe. Many of the idealists of the western world were jolted by the train of events, and everyone was desperately searching for meaning in life and an acceptable explanation for the insane brutalities issuing from the gas chambers of Hitler's Germany.

The secondary source of interest in the Christian view of history is the "problem of history" in Old and New Testament studies and theology. This field of study has always been regarded as "troublesome." Since the 1940's it has attracted the attention of some of the ablest Christian thinkers. A good example of the Christian worker toiling at this end of the theological vineyard is Rudolph Bultmann. He has been noted for his tendency to minimize the importance of history to faith by affirming a radical difference between the Christ of history and the historical Jesus. Bultmann embraces the existentialist philosophy and uses it to articulate his opposition to the liberal-positivist view that prevailed before. In his *Presence of Eternity: History and Eschatology* (1957), which is the most representative of his writings, he maintains that the descent of Christ into human flesh was meta-historical and metatemporal, and that in the faith of the Christian believer, time and world's history are overcome.[94]

In concluding this section of the chapter, I should say that the Barthian movement was a reaction to the excesses and failures of liberalism. His provocative prescription for the anxious followers of Christ triggered a series of intellectual debates in the Roman Catholic, Protestant and Orthodox churches of Christendom. Each tradition within the church tried to come up with the right answers to comfort its membership. The issues were too significant to be overlooked and too explosive to be left to the uninitiated. Reading through the volume edited and introduced by Professor McIntire, one comes to the conclusion that the search for meaning in life, at least within the Western branch of Christendom, is being carried out by many devoted thinkers and the fruits of their labors are likely to contribute to the better understanding of the Christian view of man and to the spiritual comfort and security of those Christians who are being buffeted here and there by the waves of historical uncertainty and existential anxiety. Such a galaxy of scholars includes names like Christopher Dawson, Kenneth Scott Latourette, Reinhold Niebuhr, Emil Brunner, Rudolph Bultmann, Wolfhart Pennerberg, Gustavo Gutierrez, Paul Tillich, Arnold Toynbee, Karl Barth and Jacques Maritain. This list is by no means a complete one for there are many intellectual laborers in the vast theological field and their products are available in most libraries.

A. 2. The Christian Missionary and the Diffusion of Christianity in Africa.

The arrival of Christianity on the African continent preceded the advent of Western European colonialism of recent centuries. The words of the Christian gospels reached the ears of Africans over a thousand years before the first European Christian father ventured into what they called, in church circles, the "Dark Continent."[95]

Christianity, in other words, was a religion known to some segment of Africa's population. These early Christians were mainly confined in the northern and northeastern parts of Africa. Because of this limited range of the early church in Africa and because of its regional character during the period concerned, I feel it unnecessary to go any further with the matter.[96] Instead I would proceed with my accounts of the planting of Christianity, as known to the West, in sub-Saharan Africa.

The spread of modern Christianity in the African continent could now be traced back to the pioneering efforts of Prince Henry the Navigator. It was indeed the fruits of his labor that made it possible for the Christian kingdoms to the north of Africa to venture south. By their bold ventures these exploring Christians came into contact with Africans. Some became traders and merchants plying goods from European ports, while others engaged themselves in the services of the church. Many of these men risked their lives to serve as chaplains on board exploring vessels or settled in one of the forts set up by the Portuguese authorities.

By 1500 the Christian missionaries succeeded in spreading their gospels in several African courts, including those of Benin and Congo.[97] In fact, in Congo the missionaries were so successful that the King's son became a priest after receiving training in Portugal. Added to this successful conversion of a young African prince was the drive by the Jesuits to gain a foothold in Central Africa. By the mid-seventeenth century the Jesuits had established a monastery in Sao Paulo de Loanda which had displaced San Salvador as Congo's capital. This building, however, was just a part of the Jesuits' efforts to extend their sphere of influence into what is now called Zimbabwe.

These Portuguese efforts at proselytization came to naught by the end of the eighteenth century. Though many reasons have now been given to explain away this Christian failure to expand, the fact still remains that modern Christianity did not gain ground until the beginning of the nineteenth century. Unlike the first phase of Christian expansion in Africa, this second phase was largely the labor of the Protestant churches. These churches came to Africa with enthusiasm and motivation. Their missionaries were often convinced that success is the result of persistent advocacy.

Another aspect of the planting of Christianity in Africa is the fact that this religion was promoted also by the colony of non-White settlers from the ex-slaves of the New World. These men and women were useful propagators because many among them were not unfamiliar with the teachings of Christ. Those who were not so familiar were instructed by accompanying chaplains and preachers from Nova Scotia, Jamaica, or any place where these enslaved blacks ever lived.

It was indeed this group of liberated slaves who found their way to Sierra Leone that helped convert many of the other slaves who were seized by British naval vessels in enforcement of their government's anti-slavery policies.

Within less than half a century, Christianity found converts in the Gambia, Gold Coast (now Ghana), Nigeria, Sierra Leone, and Dahomey. This development was the result of the missionary activities of liberated Africans from Sierra Leone and visiting missionaries from western countries and America.

The fold of Christianity increased when, in 1822, Liberia was offered to liberated blacks in America as a haven. This open door policy of allowing all interested U.S. blacks to emigrate to Liberia led to the arrival and establishment of many different churches which, in the main, reflected the background of the settlers in the colony. Though the founding of Monrovia proved useful in the expansion of Christianity in West Africa, its significance as well as its importance in the propagation of the faith of Christ cannot be exaggerated. If indeed we look for the source of much Christian proselytization we ought to turn our attention to Freetown, a coastal town with a natural harbor for international traffic in goods and ideas.

The most active Christian missionary groups in the 1890's were the Basle mission, the Church Missionary Society, (C.M.S.) with its many continental agents, and the Wesleyan Methodist Missionary Society. Though those bodies entered the African continent with great enthusiasm they paid heavy tolls for their invasion of Africa's landscape. Many of their missionaries perished after a brief sojourn in what came to be called the "white man's grave." For example, in the first twelve years of its work starting from 1823 at Christianborg, Accra, the Basle Mission lost eight out of nine men from fever. The C.M.S. lost fifty-three men and women in Sierra Leona between 1804 and 1824. The Methodists in the fifteen years after 1835 dispatched a total of seventy-eight missionaries, both men and women, but thirty of these died within a year of arrival.

This heavy toll on the missionaries was not felt by the Protestant churches alone. The Roman Catholic priests who became the African agents of the Roman Catholic Society of African Missions in 1859 and after, soon suffered from the same evils of malaria and yellow fever. So heavy was this toll that not a single year passed without a burial for one of the Christian missionaries.

Christian beginnings in Southern Africa were roughly contemporary with those on the West Coast. The major propagators in this corner of Africa were the German Muravians and the London Missionary Society, a body supported largely by the Congregational churches. These were later joined by the British Methodists, the Paris Evangelical Missionary Society, German Lutherans and American Congregationalists.

In 1797, the London Missionary Society began to plant itself in Southern Africa; starting from Namaqualand, this Christian group pushed on to Bechuanaland (now called the Republic of Botswana) and Rhodesia. Its proselytes soon distinguished themselves by founding a string of schools in Zulu and Xhosa country. These schools quickly came to the *loci operandi* of the missionary families living together in such settlements. Using these schools as a useful platform to educate the Africans on the teachings of Christ, these missionaries gradually estab-

lished the mission as the distinctive characteristic of Christian missionary life in Southern Africa.

In retrospect we can say that it was from these mission stations that
Christianity spread northward. In fact, many students of Southern
African history have noted that such mission stations christianized the
African peoples north of the Limpopo long before the activities of Cecil
Rhodes brought the area within the British imperial orbit. This early
success of the Church in South-Central Africa was not only due to the
activities of the missionaries but also to the services of the Zulu and
Xhosa Christians accompanying these missionaries.

The Christian propagation drive, however, began in East Africa in
1844, when the German missionaries became the first to seek converts in
Zanzibar. As servants of the Church Missionary Society, they tried
their luck in Zanzibar and then proceeded to the East African mainland
through Mombasa. After over thirty-three years of service in East
Africa, the C.M.S. entered Uganda to launch their campaign for Christianity. Despite several setbacks in the early period, Christian missionaries made significant inroads in Buganda, and by 1894, when British
imperial rule was finally imposed, Christianity had already established
itself as the religion of the Kabaka court and the chiefs of surrounding
districts.

In Central Africa the Christian penetration was spearheaded by the
Baptist Missionary School. It entered the Congo (now called Zaire) in
1870. Soon after, a host of independent missionaries flowed into the
area. These independent propagators of the Christian faith finally
decided to coalesce and form the Interdenominational Societies. One of
these, the Livingstone Inland Mission of 1878, later changed its name to
the Congo Bololo Mission, now the Regions Beyond Missionary Union.
Between 1844 and 1866 two other evangelical bodies came on the scene.
They were the Christian and Missionary Alliance and the Plymouth
Brethren respectively.

These missions were able to gain foothold in the Congo because of
their motivation and drive, and also because of the agreeable terms of
the Berlin Conference of 1884-85, which ruled that there should be no
discrimination between the religious and scientific or charitable institutions. It is indeed interesting to note that such a provision in the Berlin
Conference's agreements allowed King Leopold to make use of Arab-
Muslim traders. These men were used by Leopold to extend his control

over difficult and unreachable areas towards the Sudanese border.

Another point of interest to us should be the reemergence of Catholic missionary groups in Africa in the 1890's. As already stated above, Catholic missionaries were the first to set foot on African soil in the early period of Portuguese exploration of the African coast. They failed to consolidate their gains in Africa after the decline and fall of Portuguese and Spanish power, and consequently much of what they arduously tried to build in Africa fell to the ground.

Things began to change for the Catholic missionaries in the early 1800's. Members of the French Holy Ghost Fathers went to Senegal in 1843, and in Congo, and Angola in 1866. Catholic activities also began in 1849 in the small British colony of Bathurst (Gambia), where French nuns operated a small dispensary. The labors of the French Holy Ghost Father were soon imitated by members of the Lyons Society of African Mission, whose tragic experience in 1859 in the West African port of Freetown spurred it on to compete fiercely with the Protestant groups in West Africa. As already pointed out, the White Fathers found their way from North Africa to Tanganyika (now called Tanzania), and from there to Uganda. At the same time that they sought foothold in the east they ventured towards West Africa.

When King Leopold became the sole master of the Congo he found it useful and politic to include Catholics among the missionaries seeking his protection while recruiting converts in the field. The Scheutveld Fathers, the Order of the Sacred Heart of Mary, were allowed to propagate the Catholic faith in the Congo in 1888. They were joined four years later by the agents of the Society of Jesus. Further to the south in what we today call the Republic of South Africa, the oblates of Mary the Immaculate had already begun their mission in 1854, and in 1854 the southwest part of Southern Africa became another area of operation for the Catholic missionaries from the oblates of St. Francis de Sales. These two groups were later joined by other Christian groups in the long and arduous task of planting Christianity in Africa.

These Catholic ventures have proved to be very successful in Catholic eyes. The rapidity with which the Catholic message spread around the African continent has indeed intrigued many Protestant writers on the subject. It is commonly known that by 1900, when the colonial system in Africa was already installed for European imperialists to lubricate and operate, the Catholic church had nearly 2 million adherents. This figure climbed up to 5 million in 1930, and to 27 million in 1967, when T.A. Beetham wrote his *Christianity and the New Africa*. The Catholic Church, in a study published simultaneously in London, Dublin, and Melbourne, says that: "the Church, without any attempt to describe her presence and her expansion in Africa in purely mathematical terms, may assert that in 35 years (from 1930-1965) the number of Catholics rose from 6 to 30 million."[98] Catholic observers of the African religious scene seem to be very optimistic about the future, and rather than adopting a crusading spirit they have counselled their African representatives to be patient, prudent, shrewd, and courageous in their evangelism. Such qualities, church fathers believe, will enable Catholics to win more converts and then consolidate their African holdings.

Many reasons have been offered for the Catholic progress in Africa. Some missionaries have argued that the Catholics' late arrival in the religious scramble for Africa allowed them to profit from the blunders of the Protestant groups that had previously spent several years cultivating the fields for African converts. Others have cited the significant fact that the second Catholic drive to plant the Church doctrines differed considerably from the first in that it took place at a time when medical research on the deadly tropical diseases had advanced to the point of final liquidation. Added to this was the fact that the Church was also able to draw on the available supply of manpower in Ireland, France and Belgium. Last but not least on this point, it should be noted that many of the fifty or more different Catholic orders in Africa limited their areas of operation to the African continent.[99] This concentrated but widespread Catholic effort at proselytization gave the Church a distinct advantage over the Protestant missions.

When Africa finally came under colonial rule, the European missionary found himself in a very difficult position. Though protected by the colonial regime from the attacks and harassments of an unruly population somewhere within the newly established colony, his national and racial association with those manning the colonial apparatus soon exposed him to African suspicion and hostility.

Another area of difficulty for the missionary was the colonial regime's imposition of restrictions on the movement of missionaries in the colony. Such restrictions were in effect only in the Protectorates where some form of indirect rule was allowed to develop. The most striking example in Africa of this practice was northern Nigeria, where the Emirs exercised power under British supervision. In these parts of the old British Empire, Christian missionaries were told to keep away.

This policy of indirect rule, which had as its leading theoretician a British colonial administrator called Lugard, contributed a great deal to the educational disparity between African Christians and African Muslims. In taking note of the fact that the missionary churches were the chief agencies for the diffusion of western education in Africa, even after colonialism became the dominant order, Ali A. Mazrui has recently argued in his book *The Political Sociology of the English Language,* that the English-speaking missionaries were partly unsuccessful in propagating their religion because, in the eyes of many simple African Muslims, Christianity and English were synonymous. This idea was most evident in areas where colonial policy forbade the missionaries from entering Muslim areas. Mazrui, in continuation of his contention, has argued that Muslim suspicion of the Christian missionary gave rise to their resultant fears of the English language. Consequently, Mazrui added, indirect rule helped increase these fears; for "if Lugard did not succeed in denying Africa the English language, he certainly did succeed in slowing down its spread in the Muslim areas he controlled."[100]

The argument of Mazrui must not be dismissed off-handedly as a wild hypothesis of an African scholar. Rather, it should be looked into and seen for what it is worth. In my view, Mazrui is definitely correct in suggesting that indirect rule slowed down the pace of Christian penetration of Muslim areas and that such a system also gave political protection to those who wished to keep the language of the Nasaran (the Christian) missionary from gaining a hold over the Muslim population. My only objection to Mazrui's argument is that a careful study of the problem throughout the continent may reveal that Muslims generally were less concerned about the medium of communication used by the missionary than about the content of his message. Muslim elders, it should be pointed out, objected earlier to western education, not because such a tradition of education utilized a different language, but because it purveyed a doctrine of *Shirk* (creating partners for *Allah.*)

The polylingual character of African society exposes Mazrui's proposition to critical scrutiny, although I would hasten to add that a final answer to the question raised in Mazrui's proposition will not come before a careful study of individual Muslim societies in Africa is carried out.

To return to the earlier point about the missionary's role in the dissemination of western education I would argue that, up to the time when colonial governments decided to enter the field of African education, almost all schools were built and run by missionaries. Because of this pervasive and significant role of Christian missionaries in Africa, African history during the last century has witnessed the rise and fall of men whose intellectual garments as well as their performances in the African drama were largely the results of missionary labors. Men like Kwame Nkrumah and Leopold Senghor may be celebrated in some African quarters as leaders of African freedom, but at the same time it could be asserted that their world view and rhetoric were very much flavored by the language of the purveyors of the Abrahamic heritage. Indeed, in the language of Ali A. Mazrui, these men after going through the schools of the Christian missionaries became perfect acculturates of Western culture.[101] In other words, their education in the schools of the Christian missionaries converted them into cultural mulattoes who have assimilated well the culture of the western imperialist rulers. [102]

Missionary activity in Africa has continued even after independence. Though the missionary suffered many setbacks during the transition from colonial rule to independence because of his connections and associations with the colonial regime, events of the last decade have shown that the Christian church as a whole has adjusted to realities in Africa. Though many African nationalists have not been very satisfied with Christianity's performance in Africa, the fact remains that both missionaries and their African supporters are now aware of the weaknesses of the Church in Africa. These missionaries, I would like to emphasize very strongly, are now themselves articulating the long disputed grievances of African members of the Church. They know full well that the Africanization of church leadership is inevitable, and that Christianity's future will be a bleak one if African man is not allowed to weave a form of African Christianity that is not destructive of the African personality. In other words, Christian missionaries working in African lands are more tolerant and accommodating, and their new spirit of evangelism has opened doors of cooperation which were effectually closed when their more intolerant brethren tried to run down the African's throat an undigested Christianity which is more European than Christian.

These new attitudes cannot be described as universal, but in concluding this portion of the study we can argue that the Christian missions will continue to play a useful role in African societies so long as African, pride and dignity are not violated in the name of a bogus Christianity that is based on the cultural superiority of its alien promoters. If, however, the missionaries remain adamant and deny Africans not only effective leadership role but also opportunities to reconcile their faith with their historical past, the separatist churches will mushroom across the continent.

A. 3. The Impact of the Euro-Christian on the African World View

The advent of Christianity in Africa certainly had a wide ranging effect on African life and culture. If we define a civilization as the totality of values and material products produced by a community of men who have learned over a long period of time to live together and share common ideas about the nature of the world, about man's role in the world and about his destiny in the human drama, then we can say that the arrival of Christian missionaries constituted a direct challenge to traditional African civilization. Though there is great debate among scholars about the Christian influence in Africa, the fact remains that African life has undergone some changes as a result of missionary labors.[104]

The first and most significant area of influence was the classroom where the missionary teacher taught the alphabets to young and older Africans in search of knowledge about their gospels. This *locus operandi* of the Christian churches has indeed served the cause of Christianity well, for it has helped not only in the secular education and training of young Africans but also in the inculation of Christian values. Such an educational system provided at first instruction on the Bible only, but later on, as the colonial regime expanded its state-building activities, the three R's and the grammar of the colonial language became part of the curriculum. Such courses were included with the distinct understanding that the graduates so produced by such missionary schools would be serving the new colonial masters in the capacity of junior clerks in the budding civil service and commercial houses.

Because of this important development in the curriculum of missionary schools, African children soon found themselves learning the culture and manners of their European teachers and rulers. This deliberate process of Christian education, in other words, soon turned out to be the method by which the African was being inducted into western culture. This process was bound to have some effect, for it not only made the African the student of Christian catechism, but it also made him an imitator of western culture. This relationship was made all the more advantageous to the European missionary because the material and social universe within which the transaction occurred was under the full control of the colonial master without whose blessings the missionary could not carry on his education program for the African.

Added to the fact that the education process received the political patronage of the colonial rulers was also the fact that the mental and intellectual transformation performed by the teachers in the missionary schools had serious implications for the traditional values of the African converts. For the gradual imbibing of western values in the guise of Christian education only made the young African students victims and purveyors of that secularist materialism which has, to the dismay of Christian divines, successfully infiltrated all forms of education from the West.

This aspect of missionary education in Africa has had some very drastic effects on African life. It has ushered in a train of consequences which the early missionaries and colonial administrators were not clever enough to foresee. Not only have these secularistic elements in the missionary schools created an untrue image of Western material affluence, but they have also heightened many an African's cravings for Western goods. In fact, the pictures of European life conveyed by the school textbooks portrayed Christian Europe as a material paradise, and many young men ventured to Europe and other parts of the Western world in search of the promised land of milk and honey.

Another evidence of distinctively Christian influence is the presence of Christian churches in almost all major towns in sub-Saharan Africa. Such buildings for Sunday worship and for other scheduled activities of African Christians were constructed either in the early stages of missionary work or during the period of consolidation. The new routine which the Church introduced in African society makes church life a major factor which now differentiates the African Christian from both his Muslim neighbors and his traditional brethren. These Christian churches have brought about a form of social grouping previously unknown in Old Africa.[105] As a result of the proliferation of churches in Africa, Christians worship together in greater numbers in their own buildings, and conduct or supervise such other routine activities as Sunday schools for their children, special classes for catechumens, periodical meetings for women, concerts and picnics for the school-going age groups. In these and various other ways people professing Christianity now share interests and activities that cut across the traditional pattern of social life and distinguish them as a separate section of the tribe. In addition, it should be pointed out that African Christians have in many cases accepted special rules of conducts which are certainly new features in African life. Though writers like Melville J. Herskovits could claim that separatist movements within the Christian fold in Africa demonstrate the power and persistence of the traditional world view, the fact remains that the Christian Church is a reality in African life and the life of the middle class Christian devotee is as much affected by the church rules of conduct as his counterpart in the West.[106] The only major difference between the African Christian and his fellow Christian in Europe is the fact that, in the case of the latter, his society had already successfully reinterpreted and reintegrated Christianity, and much of what is now peddled as the way are old heresies passing off as orthodoxies.

That the church has made inroads in the abolition of certain traditional practices cannot be denied, although I would hasten to add that, as a result of the independence struggle in Africa, many African Christians as well as their missionary colleagues have shown some willingness to accommodate some of the practices frowned upon in earlier days. Whether this is a tactical move on the part of the church leaders in Africa is an open question. In my view, the fact that educated African Christians have adopted, consciously or unconsciously, many of the rules of conduct taught in missionary schools means a great deal. By embracing this aspect of church practice many of Africa's middle class families are beginning to measure themselves up to the inherited standard; those who have failed to live up to expectations are not necessarily less committed to the church standard, but are in fact the victims of the cultural paradox that is characteristic of the Christian education of the

Western missionaries. To put this point in another way, I should say that African noncompliance with church rules of conduct, or their return to traditional mode of living, is the result of the chaotic conditions created by the secularism ushered in by colonial rule and missionary education.

Except for their special activities and obligations, Christians in Africa are generally not a socially distinct group. Distinctions or residential separation exist only in exceptional cases, such as the Sabung Gari (strangers' quarters) in Northern Nigeria, where Ibos and other non-Muslims in Hausaland live. In East Africa I have learned that social intercourse between Christian and Muslim is limited. This is understandable because of the demographic and socio-economic factors peculiar to certain parts of that area. Yet, in fairness to African Christianity, one cannot deny the social accessibility of its missionaries.

Missionary activity has had another significant effect in the life of African societies. The missions were solely responsible for the intellectual conservation of many African languages and folklores. Not only did the early missionaries study the languages of their new converts, but they also thought out ways of developing orthographies for these languages. It was through their dedication and interest that languages like Yoruba have made a remarkable progress over the last century. Besides their contributions in language development, missionaries from the Euro-Christian world opened hospitals and clinics to treat wounded or diseased Africans. Two of the most celebrated pioneers in this field were Doctor David Livingstone and Doctor Albert Schweitzer.

The Euro-Christian influence on African life was also evident in three other areas. The first was the domain of intellectual life. We have learned from many writers on Africa that in the early period of missionary activity many an African chief found in the missionary a useful secretary who could reduce his chiefly thoughts to writing whenever his state wished to establish contacts with other parties. This relationship between the missionary and the African chief lasted over many years and it became very useful for the chief after colonial rule came to all Africa.

Another area of African life influenced by the Euro-Christian missionary is the cultural homogeneity of its converts. In some instances Christianization has brought uniformity among the peoples of a given country in Africa. For example, in that part of Botswana where the Tswana live, all Christians among the Ngwato, Kwena, Ngwaketse and

Tswana belong to the London Missionary Society.[107] This has helped in the social unity of the church members.

The third area where Euro-Christian influence is evident is in technological and ontological thought. The Christianization of Africans has introduced a few very important elements of thought that were never accepted in the past. Among these is the belief in a resurrection and salvation. An African theologian steeped in the theological language of the Euro-Christian gospel of Christ has told us that there is no Endzeit (the end) in traditional African thought and that "this empty area of African thought . . . should readily be filled up with the Christian concepts of the 'Endzeit,' "because "In Christ death is vanquished; the separation between God and man is forever bridged in his Incarnation."[108]

That the missionaries from western countries have penetrated the mental world of the African is proven by the widespread acceptance among African Christians of Christ (a man God) as a savior. That the idea has sunk in to many African heads, and that its implication for Africa's future are numerous could be deduced from the conclusion of J. S. Mbiti, who wrote with great seriousness that:

> Our forefathers found no myths for the *Endzeit*, however much they might have wished to find them. The New Testament supplies this missing link, not for the sake of mythology, but because the Incarnation makes it inevitable. We have to transmit this message: Africa's broken rope between Heaven and Earth is once and for all reestablished in Christ; Africa's God who evidently withdrew from men to the heavens has now come "down" to man, not only as the Son of God but also as Immanuel, God with us; and Death which came so early into man's existence from which there was no escape, is now forever abolished.[109]

In concluding this section I would say that the African man has undergone a radical change since the arrival of the missionary in Africa. This transformation has taken many forms and each of these forms is a symbol of Christian breakthrough in Africa. Though there is a growing body of African opinion that the Euro-Christian influence in Africa is superficial, there is reason to believe that Christianity as exported by Europe will survive the post-colonial surgery of the African revolutionaries and reformers. What, however, is going to be the form such a Christianity will take will remain a moot point until the forces of change in the African drama work themselves out.

4

NKRUMAH'S CONSCIENCISM AND SENGHOR'S NEGRITUDE:
Two Intellectual Responses to Africa's Search For Identity

The intrusion of a foreign culture into a society usually create psychological as well as psycho-cultural problems. This is more evident in cases where the receiving society is at the political and military mercy of the purveyors of alien culture. In the special case of Africa, Western colonialism — and to a lesser degree the Arab/Islamic penetration — introduced not only new patterns of thought but also new material products which later came to alter the economic relationships that had existed between the members of the African society, as well as between the outside world and the African society itself. That Africa today is facing many problems that can very accurately be described as an "identity problem" is not doubted. In fact, most of the students of African affairs who have analyzed the train of events in Africa since the 1960's have noted it in their statements and writings. African leaders themselves have talked and written about this aspect of the wider issue of post-colonial development in Africa.

Two major leaders of African thought — Nkrumah of Ghana and Senghor of Senegal — are singled out here for study. Their conception of the African problem is well known and, for this reason, I intend to see how their solutions to Africa's identity problem relate to the Abrahamic legacy; how their image of Africa squares with the ecumenicalism of the Abrahamic legacy; and how, finally, their solutions define the African's role in the wide world of multiracial humanity.

A. 1. Nkrumah's Consciencism as an Ideological Remedy

Dr. Kwame Nkrumah of Ghana is the most popular and yet the most hated African in modern history. His fame and adulation are the result of his efforts at unloading the Black man's burden, which the African's experience with Western colonialism and imperialism brought about after a long period of interracial strife and torture; they were also the psychological rewards given out by a community of Africans and blacks who saw him as a courageous leader working for the dignity, pride and collective upliftment of his race. In his biographical work on the former

75

President of Ghana, Basil Davison has suggested that Nkrumah was a man of vision who wanted to bring "a revolution that would lead to socialism and unite a continent." He added that Nkrumah's name became anathema in certain circles because of the following:

> He aroused irritation and anger outside Africa, especially in the old imperial countries . . . He greatly speeded up the whole process of decolonization, not only in Ghana but widely elsewhere. He spoke for black equality as though it were a right which needed no discussion. He took it for granted what the white man's world wished to concede as a gift, expecting gratitude; yet he was not thankful.[110]

Davison's analysis is correct, for it demonstrates very clearly why Kwame Nkrumah is now adulated by some and denounced by others. To put it briefly, one could say that all the controversy about him is only a result of his personal attempt to resolve a major problem collectively shared by all of Africa's children.

What, then, is Nkrumah's answer to the African identity question? His answer to this most important question is given in the most intellectual of his works — Consciencism. In that book the African thinker warns his fellow Africans that the face of Africa has changed considerably since the arrival of the colonialist, that African society today is not the old one, but a new society enlarged by Islamic and Euro-Christian influences. He devotes this work on how best Africa could be steered towards the path of political and economic salvation.[111]

In pursuit of this objective Nkrumah reasons that African man can project and develop the African personality only when he resolves the crisis in his conscience. This crisis, Nkrumah argues, is the result of the acculturation processes brought into being by the encroachments of foreign ideas into the African's world. Realizing that the defeat of colonialism and even neocolonialism will not result in the automatic disappearance of the imported patterns of thought and social organization, he calls for a way out.[112] His plan for Africa is to accept the march of history and not to return to a status quo ante. In other words, Nkrumah abhors any nostalgic glorification of ancient ways.

Nkrumah believes that Islamic civilization and European colonialism are both historical experiences of traditional Africa, that is, profound changes that have left lasting marks on the mind and society of African man. Because of this realization, he asks those Africans who call themselves African Socialists not to make the sad mistake of calling present African societies communalistic.[113] Such societies, in his view, are not traditional, but backward; and they are clearly in a state of disequilibrium. This confusion is the result of Africa's cultural encounter with the two forms of the Abrahamic legacy, both in the material and intellectual sense. Indeed, it can be argued that Nkrumah's solution rests upon his belief that African man will be able to assimilate successfully all the borrowed values and patterns of thought from outside, and then weave a new cultural and civilizational garment that will bear, not only the trademark of African ingenuity, but also all the best things in the baggage of scientific analysis and of cultural borrowing.[114]

In *Consicencism*, Nkrumah projects himself as an African nationalist who analyzes society from the perspective of a scientific socialist. Espousing a watered down materialist philosophy of the world he maintains that, contrary to popular opinion, history is made not necessarily by the ideas in the head of the man, but by the evolution of the production processes in his society. He argues that Africans will not be able to influence and control their development unless they are in full control of their means of production. Echoing the conventional Marxist jargon, Nkrumah insists that there is but one type of socialism.[115] He believes that the struggle is between capitalism and socialism and the Africans should join the vanguard forces fighting capitalism the world over.

After examining briefly some of the main points in Nkrumah's ideological formulations on socialism, one can then conclude that, to the author of *Consciencism*, the future of the African must be sought in the world of scientific socialism, and that the crisis in the African conscience can only be resolved by imposing an ideology which dispels disequilibrium and ushers in stability and order. Again, it could be argued that for Nkrumah, as for many other Africans, the reconciliation of Africa's diverse heritage and traditions is conceivably possible within a scientific socialist framework.

This Nkrumahist's view, however, raises many more questions than it answers. First of all, the fact that scientific socialism is based on a materialist philosophy which denies the existence of a supernatural order belies the possibility of peaceful coexistence between such a philosophy of life and the Islamic and Christian patterns of thought which Nkrumah himself recognizes as sociological facts in our modern African societies This reconciliation question is very crucial to the future of African man. Its success will depend, finally, on the intellectual juggling of African thinkers. J. S. Mbiti, for example, has suggested recently in an influential book that, "In their sober moments, Christianity and Islam could each present a theological course which demonstrates all these elements (from capitalist and socialist thoughts) into their views of man and the universe."[116] He believes that these religions should not adopt hostile attitudes towards the isms, rather their members should make use of their historical and theological resources for the harnessing of these supposedly anti-religious ideologies of the present age.

Whether Mbiti, who does not see much of a future in either Negritude or Consciencism as guides to a better future for the African Peoples, is making a wise proposal or not for the religious elements in Africa, only time can tell.

Ali A. Mazrui, however, has taken an optimistic view of this problem of religion and African identity. Writing in his *World Culture and the Black Experience*,[117] he informs us that traditional African religion is much more tolerant than other religious and belief systems like Islam and Christianity; that Nkrumah's hope of reconciliation between Africa's diverse legacies will depend upon the attitudes of the three segments toward each other; and that, based on past experiences in Africa, things will eventually sort themselves out, and that the interaction of the heritage of the Jewish Peoples with the polytheistic inheritance of the African tribes should help fulfill the ideal of the Universal Man.[118]

In concluding this section of the paper I would argue that, though Mazrui banks heavily on the tolerance of both traditional African religion and Islam, and Mbiti puts all his intellectual eggs in the resource basket of creative Christian and Islamic thinkers and reinterpreters of doctrines, there is no easy task ahead. One can only hope that sometime in the future Nkrumah's Consciencism may inspire others to pick up the challenge and concretize the unfulfilled dreams of the late champion of pan-Africanism. But whatever may happen in the future, the fact remains that Nkrumah's solution is a contradictory one, and its fragility will become evident as Africa's industrial base develops and African political consciousness drives African man to demand for more political and economic goods. There and then, it will become crystal clear that the religious component must exercise a dominant influence over and above society, if African man is not to lose that important spiritual link in the chain of African ontology. Such a religious emphasis helped in the past to define the social and ontological boundaries of African traditional man; consequently, it must be maintained, at least in spirit, if we are to escape the madhouses of unbridled socialism and of godless materialism.

.1. 2. Senghor's Negritude as a Solution to .Africa's Identity Problem

Unlike Kwame Nkrumah of Ghana, Leopold Sedar Senghor of Senegal belongs to a different school of thought. Like Aime Cesaire and Leon Damas, Senghor belongs to that intellectual *Troika* that spearheaded the movement now known as Negritude. This literary movement, which gradually took on a political character in French colonial territories, has been generally described as the French-speaking African's version of the Angolophonic pan-Africanist movement. Abiola Irele, a Nigerian writer who has written several articles on the subject, points out in a recent study that Leopold Senghor has impressed his personal stamp upon the attitudes and ideas of other Francophonic writers on Negritude, and for this and many other reasons, Negritude has developed into a distinct system of contemporary African thought. Irele adds:

> For although various and even contradictory stands can be distinguished
> in the writings of French-speaking black intellectuals, the efforts of
> Senghor over the past thirty years or so to create a unified framework of
> thought for the black man, and to lay the intellectual basis for a modern
> African identity, has come to confer upon the concept of Negritude a
> unity. Senghor has developed the concept to such an extent that while
> taking these other meanings and implications of a historical character, it
> now appears as a whole system of thought, as the national formulation of
> an African conception of the universe and of a mode of existence
> founded upon this fundamental conception.[119]

That Senghor's Negritude has become an African vision of reality is undisputed, and all careful analysts have tried to dissect and comprehend its secret meaning. What needs to be stressed here, however, is that Senghor has given his version of Negritude a distinctive stamp.

Negritude, Senghor writes, was not created by the three celebrated founding fathers of such a school; rather, it was a recognition of an already existing fact of life. To Senghor, early Negritude was indeed an instrument of liberation from a black identity crisis induced by the assimilation policy of the French colonialist. This early approval of Negritude, it is said, was motivated by the fact that French colonialism pursued a global policy of making Frenchmen and Frenchwomen out of subject peoples outside of Europe. Frantz Fanon, a black psychiatrist who worked in France and Algeria prior to his defection to the Algerian revolutionaries during their drive for independence from France, has made an excellent analysis of this period in the mental life of colonized people.[120] Though his subsequent intellectual development has driven him to oppose the Negritude school, he certainly shares with them certain points about the cultural violence of colonialism in Africa. In Fanon's view, colonialism transformed the black man into a black skin with a white mask.

To return to Senghor's conception of Negritude, I would argue that the Sengalese statesman finds the solution to the African identity problem in the cultivation and assertion of Africa's unique gift. This gift, in his view, is the African's emotionality as opposed to the European's rationality. He believes that one important factor that distinguishes the African from the other races is his "participating reason," which is at the heart of his apprehension of reality, and which also determines his world view. In his statement of the Negritude philosophy, Senghor argues that this world view consists of a belief in a hierarchy of forces animating the visible world, and all proceeding from a single vital principle of a Supra-natural order (what he terms to be *suriel.*)[121]

Here Senghor is drawing on the work of a Flemmish priest, Father Tempels, to explain why the Africans embrace the world and act as if they and the world together constitute a single whole. This cosmic embrace of the African, Senghor has argued, constitutes the spiritual framework of social organization in Africa. The African belief in a universe of vital forces leads him to the conclusion that history and life need not necessarily be conflictive. To Senghor, Africa's social universe is the projection into the human realm of the mystical world of vital forces.[122]

Because of this understanding of the African identity by Senghor, he has come to be described as an exponent of the primacy of culture in the field of African development. Such a view is strengthened by Senghor's own writings. He has written that culture, in contrast to civilization, is a dynamic concept which raises the very important issue of man's purpose in life and on earth. He has also remarked that: "Culture is not an appendage of politics, which one may cut without damage. It is not even a simple means of politics, culture is the prerequisite and the end of all politics deserving that name."[123]

This general outlook of Senghor gives rise to numerous and important theoretical points which together have differentiated his solution to

Africa's identity problem from Kwame Nkrumah's.[124] As should be clear from the foregoing discussion, Leopold Senghor of Senegal shared with the late Nkrumah the common belief in the unity of Africa and the common feeling that an anticipated system of thought ought to be developed to dignify and strengthen the African's claim for a seat at the banquet of civilizations. Yet the two men were worlds apart. Whereas Senghor focuses on culture and believes that Africa's salvation lies in the development of Africa's culture, which is the guiding spirit of civilization and the very texture of society, Nkrumah, on the other hand, admonishes his fellow Africans to seek political kingdom. By the political kingdom Nkrumah means the capturing of political independence from the colonial powers. He is of the belief that the attempt to modernize African societies without any sign of full political independence is a futile venture; for economic independence, which in Nkrumah's view is the stepping stone to cultural freedom and independence, is inconceivable without political independence.

This difference of opinion between Senghor and Nkrumah has led the two men to take antipodal positions on many important issues facing the African man.[125] For example, on the issue of economic development, Senghor, who is a champion of African cultural values in all African political debates on Africa's identity in the world, has opted for what he calls African Socialism. In developing this theory he has argued in criticism of Marxism that, though Marxism claims to be a universal gospel applicable to all mankind, it is a Eurocentric outfit because it has profited a European proletariat which feeds on the same colonial body as the European bourgeoisie. Senghor goes two steps further by denouncing Marxist/Leninism as a godless materialism whose relevance to modern life has been grossly undermined by the advance in scientific knowledge. Such an advance, he maintains, has not only proven the Marxist wrong, but has also demonstrated to Europe that Africa's traditional approach to knowledge, which he characterized as sympathetic, intuitive and sympathetic, was very much compatible with the latest theories of science in the West.

Writes Senghor, African Socialism is the best way to solve Africa's problems. He sees in such a philosophy the way out of current difficulties in African society, and he believes that traditional African values will lay the foundation of the new society we wish to fashion out of the materials left behind by the colonialists. He put across this important point when he wrote the following passage some time ago:

> We have chosen the African way to Socialism, which will be a synthesis
> of Negro-African cultural values, of Western methodological and spirit-
> ual values, and socialist technical and social values. Man is a constant
> factor in all our calculations, we want to make him happier by setting
> him free from contradictions and from all forms of slavery; we want to
> put an end to his "alienation" in the real world.[126]

In spite of his strong emphasis on African cultural values Senghor has,
however, tended to be an advocate of universalism. Feeding on the ideas
of the Jesuit Philosopher-Scientist, Pierre Tielhard de Chardin, Senghor
has come to express the view that his ideal is the creation of the
civilization of the universal. He has repeatedly argued that such a world
civilization could only become a reality when all the constituent civilizations in the world are allowed to make their own contributions. He
maintains that Europe and Africa each has her own tradition of civilization development and each must make the contributions for which she is
best equipped. This complementarity of civilizations, Senghor adds, is
the basis for the gradual emergence of the true humanity.

Such an understanding of the human experience has accounted for
Senghor's controversiality in African circles. It has led him to say, quite
sincerely, that judged from the wider perspective of history, colonialism was not necessarily totally evil, without any benefits for Africans.
Again, Senghor's view of world history also differentiates him from
men like Nkrumah, and from Sekou Toure who sees his brother
Senghor as a reactionary politician playing consciously or unconsciously into the hands of the neocolonialists.

5

CONCLUSIONS

*A*s the previous sections of this work have already revealed, the thrust of my argument has been that African man is now confronted by three competing world views, two of which are offshoots of the Abrahamic tradition. Throughout this study I have tried to demonstrate the main features of the encounter between Africa and the Abrahamic tradition, as preached and practiced by Muslims and Christians respectively. This attempt at clarification was made so as to identify the differences between traditional Africa's cosmology and the Abrahamic understanding of reality and man's role and place in the whole scheme. Added to my endeavor to specify differences between the values of old Africa and the two versions of the Abrahamic tradition in Africa, is the fact that I made another attempt to examine the thoughts of two articulate Africans — Kwame Nkrumah and Leopold Senghor —whose writings are widely read by Africans and, in most cases, are likely to help in the final resolution of the cultural schizophrenia which is characteristic of many children in Africa today.

In concluding this study I would maintain that the advent of both Islam and Euro-Christianity has had a traumatic effect on the Africans, who are now embracing these two faiths. That both of these religions have come to stay in Africa for good is known to almost everyone. The Muslims, it seems, have been on the scene for a thousand years. The Christians have also been in contact with Africans for over a thousand years.

The findings of this study can be summarized in the following manner:

First of all, it should be pointed out that a correct picture of Africa's present attempt to forge a new identity will be obtained only after we have learned to identify the problems of culture development in Africa today. By looking into each of the three religions separately one may be able to analyze the differences, and to see how best the African Conscience could be developed to serve African man in this crucial post-independence period. This examination of the old Africa's religion and the two versions of the Abrahamic tradition suggests that African man must assimilate the cultural values of these traditions correctly if he really intends to have influence on the course of world history. Without being thoroughly digested these elements of the Abrahamic tradition will be terribly distorted and the unifying character of their ecumenical doctrines will be lost. This is especially true now that the African wishes to impress upon the world both his right to be different and his determination to be a celebrated participant at the banquet of civilizations.

Another point which needs to be emphasized in this concluding section is the fact that the Abrahamic tradition has taken three distinct forms in history: namely, the Jewish, the Christian and the Islamic. Each of these forms has made a contribution in human history and each at one point or another has been championed by one nation or tribe, and in so doing, brought fame, glory, and power to it.

The Jewish people came out of bondage in Pharaonic Egypt because of the liberating message of Moses, who was a stammering Prophet chosen to echo the Abrahamic tradition right in the heartland of Pharaoh's kingdom. That Moses succeeded in humiliating the oppressive Pharoah is well known, but what is often overlooked is this Biblical story is the fact that Moses was a strong advocate of a tradition which believes not only in the freedom of the body of man but also that of his mind. This story, I am inclined to argue, demonstrates that Africans, working within the framework of the Abrahamic tradition, could very well draw out parallels from other, and older, custodians of the Abrahamic tradition. Within the context of our present world such an exercise would not only make the African believer very optimistic, but would also impress upon him not to be so *oppressed* by man as to *forget* the divine mission thrust upon him.

Again, by the same token, we can also say that the African could also relate his adoption of Abrahamic religion to that of the founding fathers of the early Christian church, who were not only lucky to be born Jews, but faithful enough to transform the milk of human kindness and faith in God into the more unifying blood of their Christian savior. Indeed, such was the faith of these early followers of Jesus that the Roman empire which persecuted them at one time could be captured in the net of Christian prudence. All this history of the early Christian church, I would argue, constitutes an important lesson for African man. The African not only stands a chance, in his present condition of being a

believer assimilating the Abrahamic tradition into his culture, of effect-
ing the most admirable synthesis, but he may very well succeed where
the European custodian of such a tradition has failed. This is to say that
Africa's supposedly negative condition of late-comerism may well turn
out to her advantage. After having experimented with an ontology and
a cosmology which stress human harmony and cosmic orderliness for
over a million years, and now assuming the position of a custodian of the
Abrahamic tradition in a world of dehumanizing technology and frag-
mented personalities, couldn't it be said for Africa that her children
have mounted once again the stage of global history during what could
turn out to be the beginning of the best period in the human drama? In
the eyes of Christian Africans, a successful synthesis of their Savior's
doctrine of ecumenical love and brotherhood, with the scientific and
technological heritage of the modern world, may well transform the
peoples of their continent from being the *Wretched of the Earth* into the
salt and humanizing elements of the earth. And all of this would come
about not within the framework of a narrow nationalism, but within
the best tradition of Abraham, whose faith in God as well as his standing
with Him combined to confer upon his seeds within humanity, the
mantle of leadership. Indeed, is it not true that since the appearance of
Christianity, Judaism and Islam on the world scene, custodians of the
Abrahamic tradition have enjoyed the privilege of playing the role of
major actors in the human drama?

   This aspect of the Abrahamic legacy was best illustrated by the
miraculous rise of Islam. This civilization, which has yet to be understood in all its dimensions, catapulted an unknown people into historical
prominence within a very short time. In my view, the miracle of the
Prophet Muhammed was not necessarily his success in destroying established empires around his homeland, but the fact that he reaped a
wonderful harvest from the minds and labors of an unorganized Arab
people, simply by capitalizing on the mesmerizing powers of the Arabic
language and the beauty and mystery of a Divine message similar to that
of the Prophet Abraham. The Arab experience under Islam also has a
lesson for Africa: that is, it shows man that the spoken word is power
and that the divine presence is paradoxically most visible in words
rather than in objects. The Arab experience provides food for thought
to those Africans who can draw shrewd conclusions.

   After pointing out the various parallels between the African experience and that of other peoples' history has dignified by making them custodians of the Abrahamic tradition, I now proceed to the third finding of this paper. This study, I would again argue, reveals that the Abrahamic tradition came to Africa with men committed to trade and to the use of the written word. What this aspect of the Abrahamic tradition reveals is that such a tradition encourages the creation of cities and temples, for one distinctive characteristic of a literate society is its tendency to use the written word to control human bodies, hence, material civilization.

This is an important point about the Abrahamic tradition and we need to relate it to the dominant values of traditional African civilization to see how the modern African is at pains to keep his balance while walking on the tightrope of civilizational reconciliation. That cities and books open new vistas and raise new hopes for man is not doubted; what remain a problem for traditional African man, however, are his pains at reconciling the psycho-cultural and psycho-historical differences in attitudes and beliefs created by an encounter between the *old way* and the *new way*.

I am of the opinion that the Abrahamic vision can be reconciled with the traditional African's view of life, provided that we allow African man's resilience to take its course. This will come about when the African man sees that the Abrahamic tradition itself is a tripartite soul that rides three different horses, and each horse wishes to be adorned with the ribbon of superiority. The Jewish, Christian and Islamic forms of such a tradition are all derived from the same source, but their theological claims have set them apart. The first claims for its members the exclusive status of historical and transhistorical importance denied to all other humans; the second, on the other hand, claims for itself the privilege of being the blessed community that testifies before all men the fact that God Himself came in the person of Jesus Christ to save humanity; and yet the third claims that its prophet was the last and that the community he founded was honored by Allah to assume the Adamite title of Caliph (God's Viceregent) on earth.

When viewed from this angle, the Abrahamic tradition becomes very clear to the traditional African, for it shows that his conversion to any one of these forms of the Abrahamic tradition can only be progressive and fruitful if he acts out his new faith and rituals within the framework of tolerance that several thousand years of experimentation with the old religion has brought about. This African achievement, if properly harnessed and utilized for the good of humanity, could constitute the most convincing evidence that Africa's presence at the banquet of civilizations is more than a gift to a generally intolerant and chauvinistic mankind.

Last but not least, I would argue that African civilization in the post-colonial era could evolve into an example of human success in a age of scepticism, cynicism and defeatism. Why do I say this? Well, the African has suffered the *enslavement* which Moses' people experienced in Egypt; he has carried the *cross* of suffering by enduring humiliation and torture because of the biological cross called color; he has waged the Jihad, in the sense that he has faced up to the challenges and dangers of his physical environment by upholding his *humanity* in spite of attempts by the racialistic branch of humanity to deny his *manhood*.

Though these analogies may not be theologically acceptable to some African believers in the Abrahamic legacy, I feel it necessary to point them out just for the sake of demonstrating that the relationship between the African traditional religion and the Abrahamic tradition is not necessarily one between unbridgeable areas of thought and action. I think my last statement should read as follows: African man, like all other men, is born to wonder about his life, his thoughts, and his world; but if he is to wonder more, while working on how to wander less in the realm of speculation, he must embrace the Abrahamic tradition and act upon it within the framework of religious tolerance developed by his ancestors. Indeed, if there is ever going to be a structure of world peace, its creators must know the secret language which traditional African man has evolved over several millennia to deal with fellow men as well as nature. This language is that of tolerance and social harmony, a medium of communication which was best symbolized in the old Africa by the drum. Such a human instrument does not stimulate and excite the mind; rather it coaxes and subdues it to join the *body* of man in the rhythmical dance of nature. The Abrahamic religions, therefore, must cultivate this language of Africa if they are to fulfill their mission in both Africa and the modern world.

FOOTNOTES

1. For some works dealing with the various positions taken by many African thinkers, see the following works: Claude Wauthier, *The Literature and Thought of Modern Africa* (New York: Praeger Publishers, 1967); Robert W. July, *The Origins of Modern African Thoughts* (New York: Frederick A. Praeger, Publishers, 1967); Kwame Nkrumah, *Consciencism* (New York: Monthly Review Press, 1965); W.A.E. Skurnik et al, *African Political Thought: Lumumba, Nkrumah, and Toure* (Denver, Colorado: University of Denver, 1967/1968); Leopold Sedar Senghor, *Liberate 1: Negritude et Humanisme* (Paris: de seuil, 1964); Mamadou Dia, *Nations Africaines et Solidarite Mondiale* (Paris: Presses Universitaires de France, 1960).

2. For details on this and related issues, see Frantz Fanon, *The Wretched of the Earth*, (New York: Grover Press, Inc., 1963).

3. See his "Christianity and the Religious Culture of Africa," in Kenneth Y. Best, edited, *African Challenge*, (Nairobi, Kenya: Trans-Africa Publishers, 1975) p. 5.

4. *Ibid.* p. 20.

5. *Ibid.* p. 17.

6. Victor Ferkiss, *Africa's Search for Identity.* (New York: George Braziller, 1966), pp. 10 & 77.

7. See Mazrui's *Towards a Pax Africana.* (London & Chicago: The University of Chicago Press, 1967), especially chapter 3.

8. See Hodgkin's "The Relevance of 'Western' Ideas for the New African States," pp. 62-63. Quoted in James S. Coleman in a chapter entitled, "Tradition and Nationalism in Tropical Africa," contained in *New States in the Modern World* (975), edited by Martin Kilson.

9. See his "Islam in the Context of Contemporary Socio-Religious Thought in Africa," in Charles Malik, edited, *God and Man in Contemporary Islamic Thought* (Beirut, Lebanon: American University of Beirut Centennial Publications, 1972) p. 16ff.

10. For some discussion on this and other related points in the context of Islam and Pan-Africanism, see my "Islam and Pan-Africanism," *L'Afrique et L'Asie Modernes*, No. 104, 1975.

11. This was a farewell speech given by Dr. Kwame Nkrumah. See *West Africa*, February 14, 1953. Quoted in *Information Digest of African Bureau*, London, No. 7, February-March, 1953, p. 4.

12. For a summary of the position of Awo, see his statement of June 21, 1961 listed as Appendix 24 in Colin Legum's *Pan-Africanism — A Short Political Guide* (Westport, Connecticut: Greenwood Press Publishers, 1976). p. 266ff.

13. John S. Mbiti, *African Religions and Philosophy* (Garden City, New York: Doubleday & Co., Inc., 1970 edn.) P. 38; E. Bolaji Idowu, *African Traditional Religion*, (Mary Knoll, New York: Orbis Boos, 1973), p. 85.

14. Mbiti, *Op Cit.*, p. 38.

15. *Ibid.* p. 119.

16. *Vincent Mulago, "Vital Participation" in Kwesi Dickson and Paul Ellingworth, Biblical Revelation and African Beliefs,* (Mary Knoll, New York: Orbis Books, 1969) p. 138.

17. Quoted by E.A. Adeolu Adegobola in his "The Theological Basis of Ethics," in Kwesi Dickson and Paul Ellingworth, *Op Cit.,* p. 117.

18. Vincent Mulago, *Op Cit.,* p. 139.

19. *Ibid.,* p. 140.

20. *Ibid.,* p. 143.

21. Claude Wauthier, *The Literature and Thought of Modern Africa* (New York: Praeger Publishers, 1967) p. 172.

2. See Amadou Hampate Ba, "African Art, where the hands have Ears," *The UNESCO Courier,* February, 1971, p. 12.

045 23. See his *Muntu — An Outline of the New African Culture,* translated by Majorie Greene (New York: Grove Press Inc., 1961) p. 105.

24. K. C. Anyanwu, "African Religion as an Experienced Reality, *Thought and Practice,* (The Journal of the Philosophical Association of Kenya), Vol. 2, No. 2, 1975, p. 156.

25. John S. Mbiti, *op. cit.,* p. 205.

26. See E. G. Parrinder, *African Traditional Religions,* (3rd edn.), New York: Harper & Row Publishers, 1970), p. 134.

27. This is a restatement of his position as presented by Janheinz Jahn in his *Muntu,* p. 106.

28. This is one of the four basic concepts Jahn borrowed from Reverend Kagame's work on Rwanda Bantu ontology. The other three concepts are Muntu, Kuntu, and Kintu. Jahn believed that all beings, all essences, in whatever form it is conceived, can be subsumed under one of these categories. Nothing can be conceived outside them. W.E. Abraham, a philosopher from Ghana, disagrees with Jahn's interpretation of African culture. See his *Mind of Africa,* (Chicago: The University of Chicago Press, 1962), p. 142.

29. Mbiti, *op. cit.,* p. 21.

30. See his "The African Experience of God, *Thought and Practice* (a Journal of the Kenyan Philosophical Society), Vol. No. 1, 1974, p. 21.

31. I use the term Western to mean the European and American states that embrace the capitalist or communist philosophies of society and life.

32. *The Holy Quran,* (translated by Yusuf Ali) Chapter 94:8.

33. *Ibid.,* Chapter 33:40.

34. *Ibid.,* Chapter 103.

35. *Ibid.,* Chapter 98:6-7.

36. This point is discussed at great length in my "The Islamic State and Economic Development: A Theoretical Analysis," *Islamic Culture,* Vol. 50, No. 1, (January, 1976). See also Kenneth Cragg, *The Privilege of Man,* (London: The Athlone Press, 1968), especially Chapter 2; Hammudah Abdalati, *Islam in Focus,* (Indianapolis, Indiana: American Trust Publications, 1975).

37. For a detailed treatment of these aspects of Islamic thought, see Frithjof Schuon, *Understanding Islam*, (London: George Allen, 1976).

38. Indeed Cheikh Anta Diop, the Senegalese historian and physicist, has argued in a controversial work that there is overwhelming evidence that the earliest inhabitants of Arabia were racially Negro and that these were later invaded by a coarse white Jectanide tribe who gradually became assimilated into Black life and culture. Diop gives credence to his claim by saying:

"These facts, on which even Arab authors agree, prove . . . that the Arab race cannot be conceived as anything but mixture of Blacks and Whites, a process continuing even today. These same facts also prove that traits common to Black culture and Semitic culture have been borrowed from the Blacks."

See his *The African Origins of Civilization: Myth or Reality*, edited and translated by Mercer Cook, (New York: Westport: Lawrence Hill & Co., 1974). pp. 123-128.

39. For a detailed account on the emergence of Islam in the Maghrib, see Bernard Lewis' brief chapter on "The Invading Crescent" in Roland Oliver, edited, *The Dawn of African History*, (London: OUP, 1969). 5th edition, Chapter 6. See also J. Spencer Trimingham, *A History of Islam in West Africa*, (London: OUP, 1975), Chapter 1; Jamil Abu Nasr, *A History of the Maghrib*, (London: OUP, 1965); E.W. Bovill, *Caravans of the Old Sahara*, (London, 1933); E.W. Bovill, *The Golden Trade of the Moors*, 2nd edition, revised and with additional material by Robin Hallet, (London & New York: OUP, 1968).

40. E.W. Bovill, *op. cit.*, p. 67.

41. Ibn Khaldun, *Histoire de Berberes*, ed. de Slane, (Algiers, 1847) Quoted by J. Spencer Trimingham, *op. cit.*, p. 18.

42. E.W. Bovill, *The Golden Trade of the Moors*.

43. Bernard Lewis, *op. cit.*, p. 34.

44. The role of the Almoravids in the diffusion of Islam in the West Sudan is still being argued among scholars. One of the leading authorities is the Israeli scholar, Nehemia Levtzion. In a recent publication he sums up his position on the role of the Almoravid in spreading Islam in the West Sudan in the following manner:

There can be little doubt that the Almoravids accelerated the Islamization of Ghana, but they did so only after the ground had been prepared through the peaceful influence of Muslim traders.

For details about the life of the founder of Almoravid movement, see Levtzion's chapter of Ibn Yasin in John Ralph Willis' edited volume, *Studies in West African Islamic History*, (London & Totowa: Frank Cass, 1979), p. 103ff.

45. J. Spencer Trimingham, *op. cit.*, p. 84.

46. E.W. Bovill, *op. cit.*, p. 84.

47. For this section of the paper, I relied heavily on John Ralph Willis' edited volume, *op. cit.*, especially his Introduction.

48. See his *The Jahanke*, (London: International African Institute, 1979), p. 7.

49. Omar Jah, "Islamic History in the West Sudan," *The Bulletin of the Islamic Center of Washington, D.C.*, , Vol. 7, No. 1. (May, 1978), p. 24. Reprinted from *The Journal of the*

Muslim World League, (January, 1978).

    50. *Ibid.,* p. 24.

    51. See Dr. Batran's Chapter in J.R. Willis', edited, *op. cit.*

    52. See R.G. Jenkins' paper in Willis' edited volume.

    53. See Norris, "The History of Shinquit, according to Idaw Ali Tradition," Bulletin I.F.A.N., XXIV, 3-4, 1962, pp. 393-403. Quoted by R.G. Jenkins, *op. cit.,* p. 1.

    54. For more information on this subject see J.D. Fage, *A History of Africa,* (New York, Alfred Knopf, 1978), Chapters 6-8, Part 2. See also his earlier work, *A History of West Africa,* (Cambridge, England: Cambridge University Press, 1959).

    55. For some interesting discussion on this subject, see Philip D. Curtin, *Economic Change in Pre-Colonial Africa, Senegambia in the Era of the Slave Trade,* (Madison, Wisconsin & London, England: University of Wisconsin Press, 1979).

    56. See Mungo Park, *Travels of Mungo Park,* edited by Roland Miller, (London, Dent, 1954).

    57. See B.G. Martin, *Muslim Brotherhoods in Nineteenth Century Africa,* (Cambridge, London, New York/Melbourne: Cambridge University Press, 1979), p. 17.

    58. Omar Jah, *op. cit.,* p. 27.

    59. For some discussion on these cultivators of Islam in West Sudan, see the respective chapters on Maba Jahu and Samori in John Ralph Willis' edited volume.

    60. For a good background on the early history of Islam in Eastern Sudan, see Yusuf Fadl Hassan, "The Penetration of Islam in Eastern Sudan," in I.W. Lewis, edited, *Islam in Tropical Africa,* (London: Oxford University Press, 1966), pp. 144-159.

    61. Yusuf Fadl Hassan, *The Arabs and The Sudan,* (Khartoun, Sudan: Khartoun University Press, 1973), p. 124.

    62. *Ibid.,* p. 125f.

    63. *Ibid.,* p. 155.

    64. J. Spencer Trimingham, *Islam in Ethiopia,* (Oxford: OUP, 1952), p. 270f.

    65. See I.W. Lewis, *op. cit.,* p. 261.

    66. See Baxter's chapter in I.W. Lewis, *op. cit.,* pp. 248-250.

    67. See his chapter on "The Coast Before the Arrival of the Portuguese" in B.A. Ogot and J.A. Kieran, edited, *ZAMANI: A Survey of East African History,"* (New York: Humanities Press, 1971), p. 107f.

    68. See F.J. Berg's paper in B.A. Ogot and J.A. Kieran, *op. cit.,* p. 139.

    69. *Ibid.*

    70. The principal route was from such ports as Bagamoyo and Sudani. The second was on the southern Tanzanian Coast, centering on such ports as Kilwa, Kivinje, Mkindani and Lindi. The third route began on the northern Tanzanian and southern Kenyan coasts, from such ports as Pangani, Tanga, and Mombasa. See Bennett's chapter in B. A. Ogot and J. A. Kieran, *op cit.,* p. 216f.

    71. Bennett, *Ibid.,* p. 236.

72. Daniel F. McCall and Norman R. Bennett, (eds.), *Aspects of West African Islam*, (Boston, Mass.: African Studies Center, Boston University, 1971), p. 17.

73. *Ibid.,* p. 17.

74. Cited in Thomas Walker Arnold, *The Preaching of Islam.* (London: Constable & Co., Ltd., 1933), p. 361.

75. I.W. Lewis, *Islam in Tropical Africa,* (London: Oxford University Press, 1969), p. 70.

76. See Nehemia Levitzion's "Patterns of Islamization in West Africa," in Daniel F. McCall and Norman R. Bennett, eds., *op. cit.*

77. M. Hiskett, "An Islamic Tradition of Reform in the West Sudan from the Sixteenth to the Eighteenth Century," *BSOSA.,* XXV, 3, (1962). See also her *The Sword of Truth* (1973) which deals with Shehu Usman Dan Fodio.

78. This view is attributed to M. Hiskett. Vladimir Klima et al. questioned the validity of such a hypothesis and they underscored their point by saying that "it is doubtful whether such an important process as the creation of a literacy in Hausa was really an instantaneous consequence of a rapid social and ideological change occurring during the Djihadi period. (They) stressed that the roots of such an important phenomenon as writing in the main language of Hausa might perhaps also be found in the long drawn-out process of interference of Hausa and Arabic into the written text produced in the area . . .(that) the revolutionary situation during eh Djihadi period might have represented only the final incentive and an impetus towards a shift in the written form of the language, the roots of which had already objectively existed in the Hausa language community for a relatively long period. For details and references on this important question, see their *Black Africa,* (Dorrecht-Holland/Boston-USA: D. Reidel Publishing Co., 1976).

79. *Ibid.*

80. Edward Blyden, *Christianity, Islam and the Negro Race,* (Edinburgh, Scotland: Edinburgh University Press, 1967), p. 187.

81. For a statement of the Christian position regarding life and man's place in the world, see M.A.C. Warren's "Opposition to Christianity," in *Twentieth Century Christianity,* (1963), edited by Bishop Stephen Neill.

82. See Arend Theodor van Leeuwen, *Christianity in World History,* (New York: Charles Scribner's Sons, 1964), p. 101.

83. *Ibid.,* p. 113.

84. *Romans,* Chapter 6, Verses 3-8.

85. *Colossians,* Chapters 3, Verses 1-3; Verse 5.

86. Eric Kahler, *The Meaning of History,* (New York: George Braziller, Inc., 1964). pp. 64-65.

87. For some interesting discussion on secularistic tendencies among Christian writers of our time, see Andrew Greeley, *Unsecular Man,* (New York: Schocken, 1972). See also Harvey Cox's *Secular City,* (New York: Macmillan Publishing Co., Inc., 1975).

88. M. C. D'Arcy, *The Meaning and Matter of History: A Christian View,* (New York: The Noonday Press, 1959), p. 98

89. *Ibid.*, p. 100.

90. For a penetrating analysis of the technical civilization in the modern western society, see Jacques Elue, *The Technological Society,* (New York: Vantage Books, 1964).

91. Karl Barth, "The Christian Belief in Providence," in C.T. McIntire, ed., *op. cit.,* pp. 205-223. See especially McIntire's brief introduction to this essay taken from Barth's monumental work.

92. W.H. Horton, "The Development of Theological Thought," in Bishop Stephen Neill's edited volume, *Twentieth Century Christianity,* (Garden City, New York: Dolphin Books, Doubleday & Co., Inc., 1963), p. 254.

93. Neill, *op. cit.,* p. 255. For a modern restatement of Christological revelation, see John Knox, *The Humanity and Divinity of Christ,* (London & New York: Cambridge University Press, 1967).

94. This work of Bultmann was published by Harper & Row Publishers, 1957.

95. For a sample of works on those two Abrahamic religions, see J. Mullen, *The Catholic Church in Modern Africa,* (London: Geoffrey Chapman, 1965); C.P. Groves, *The Planting of Christianity in Africa,* Vols. 1-4, (London: Lutterworth Press, 1958); R. Oliver, *The Missionary Factor in East Africa,* (London: Longmans, 2nd edition, 1965); T.A. Beetham, *Christianity and the New Africa,* (New York: Frederick Praeger, 1967).

96. For some discussion on early Christianity in Africa, see Tarikh (a journal of the Historical Society of Nigeria), Vol. 2, No. 1, pp. 1-77.

97. In this section I relied heavily on T.A. Beetham, *op. cit.*

98. Ernesto Gallina, *Africa Present — A Catholic Survey of Facts,* (London, Melbourne, Dublin: Geoffrey Chapman, 1970), p. 23.

99. *Ibid.*, p. 23.

100. Ali A. Mazrui, *The Political Sociology of the English Language,* (The Hague and Paris: Moulton and Co., 1975), Chapter 3.

101. For some discussion of this concept of Mazrui, see his "African Intellectuals in the 1980's: Pilgrim's Retreat and Patriot's Progress," (A paper presented at the African Studies Association Convention, Palmer House Hotel, Chicago in October-November, 1974).

102. The term cultural mulatto was used by President Leopold Senghor in one of his numerous works to describe himself.

103. For studies on these groups, see Bengt, G.M. Sundkler, *Bantu Prophets in South Africa* (London, 1948); V.E.W. Hayward (ed.), *African Independent Church Movements* (New York: Friendship Press 1965); H.W. Turner, *African Independent Church,* 2 Vols. (London and New York: Oxford University Press, 1967); See also Melville J. Herskovits, *The Human Factor in Changing Africa* (New York: Vintage Books, 1962).

104. Herskovits, *op.cit.,* Chapter 7.

105. For an example of this phenomenon, see I. Schaper's "Christianity and the Tswana," in Simon and Phoebe Ottenberg's *Cultures and Societies of Africa* (New York, Random House, 1960) pp. 489-503.

106. Melville Herkovits, *op cit.,* Chapter 14.

107. See I. Schaper's article in Simon and Phoebe Ottenberg (edited), *op. cit.*

108. J.S. Mbiti "Eschatology" in Kwesi Dickson and Paul Ellingworth, *op. cit.*, p. 184.

109. *Ibid.*, p. 184.

110. Basil Davidson, *Black Star: A View of the Life and Times of Kwame Nkrumah* (London: Allen Lane, 1973) p. 16.

111. For more details, see his *Consciencism* (New York: Monthly Review Press, 1965).

112. For a good account of Nkrumah's views on Neo-Colonialism and economic domination in Africa, see his *Neocolonialism: The Last Stage of Imperialism,* (London, 1965).

113. See Nkrumah's "African Socialism Revisited," in a booklet entitled *Two Myths* published in 1968 by Panaf publications, London. This is a reprint of an original article in *African Forum,* Vol 2., No. 3 (1966).

114. *Ibid.*, p. 9.

115. *Ibid.*, p. 7.

116. J. S. Mbiti, *African Religions and Philosophies* (New York: Doubleday & Co., Inc., 1970), p. 348.

117. Published in 1974 by Washington University Press, Seattle, Washington, U.S.A.

118. *Ibid.*, p. 34.

119. See his "Negritude Revisited," *ODU* (New Series No. 5 (April, 1971), pp. 4-5.

120. See his *Wretched of the Earth* (New York: Grove Press, 1968.)

121. Irele, *op. cit.*, p. 16.

122. See Senghor's *On African Socialism* (New York: Praeger, 1964).

123. Quoted from the proceedings of *Seminaire* (1960 by W.A.E. Skurnik in his *The Foreign Policy of Senegal* (Evanston, Illinois: Northwestern University Press 1972), pp. 194-5.

124. For a comprehensive but very critical analysis of Nkrumah's political thought, see Kenneth W. Grundy's chapter on Nkrumah in W.A. Skurnik, (edited) *African Political Thought: Lumumba, Nkrumah and Toure* (Denver, Colorado: University of Denver, 1967/68).

125. See Robert W. July, *The Origins of Modern African Thought* (New York, Praeger, 1967), pp. 473-4.

126. See his *On African Socialism,* p. 134-40.

SELECT BIBLIOGRAPHY

In writing this work, I rely heavily on other writers' more detailed studies on many aspects of African history and society. The rapidity with which the literature proliferates has made it virtually impossible for one man to read, digest and synthesize everything. This list is by no means exhaustive. It is only a selective one that identifies the numerous sources which this author finds helpful because they influence his thinking and writing on the subject. Those authors and readers who do not see their works listed here should forgive my sin of omission in the event they notice something of their own in my line of thinking.

REFERENCE AND BIBLIOGRAPHIC WORKS

Ofori, Patrick E. *Black African Traditional Religions and Philosophy: A Selected Bibliographic Survey of the Sources from the Earliest Times to 1974.* Nendlin: Kraus-Thomson,.1975.

Christianity in Tropical Africa: A Selective Annotated Bibliography, Nendlin: KTO, 1977.

Turner, Harold. *Bibliography of New Religious Movements in Primal Societies.* Vol. 1: Black Africa, Boston, Massachusetts: G.K. Hall, 1977.

The Howard University Bibliography of African and Afro-American Religious Studies: With locations in American Libraries/Compiled by Ethel L. Williams and Clifton Brown. Wilmington, Delaware: Scholarly Resources, 1977.

Zell, Hans M. *African Books in Print: An Index by Author, Title and Subject,* London, England: Marsell Information/Publishing Limited in Association with the University of Ife Press, Ile-Ife, Nigeria.

Zoghby, Samir M. *Islam in Sub-Saharan Africa, A Partially Annotated Guide,* Washington, D.C.: Library of Congress, 1978.

BOOKS

Abdalati, Hammudah. *Islam in Focus.* Indianapolis, Indiana: American Trust Publications, 1977.

Abun Nasr, Jamil. *A History of the Maghrib*. London: Oxford University Press, 1965.

Africa Wide, Christian Communications Congress, Nairobi, 1971. *Africa Wide Christian Communications Congress, Nairobi, Kenya, 14-21; March, 1971*: report/edited by C. Richard Shumaker; sponsored by African Evangelical Literature Office, (s./:s.n, between 1971 and 1974) (Kijabe, Kenya: Africa Inland Church Press).

Ahmad, Jamal M. "Islam in the Context of Contemporary Socio-Economic Thought in Africa," in Charles Malik, ed. *God and Man in Contemporary Islamic Thought*. Beirut, Lebanon: American University of Beirut Centennial Publications, 1972.

All Africa Churches Conference on Christian Education in a Changing Africa, Salisbury, Southern Rhodesia, 1963. *Christian Education in Africa;* report of a conference. London, published for the All Africa Churches Conference by the Oxford University Press, 1963.

All Africa Churches Conference, Salisbury, Southern Rhodesia, 1963. *Christian Education in Africa:* report of a conference held at Salisbury, Southern Rhodesia, 29 December 1962 to 10 January 1963. London published by the Oxford University Press, 1963.

All Africa Conference of Churches. *The Struggle Continues: Official All Africa Conference of Churches,* Lusaka, Zambia, All Africa Conference of Churches, 1975.

All Africa Conference of Churches. Refugee Department. *Training refugee today for a better tomorrow/* (Melaku Kifle), 1975.

All Africa Seminar on the Christian Home and Family Life, Kitwe, N. Rhodesia, 1963. The All African Seminar on the Christain Home and Family Life, held at Mindolo Ecumenical Centre, Kitwe, N. Rhodesia; 17 February to 10 April, 1963. The Seminar was sponsored by the All Africa Churches Conference in collaboration with the World Council of Churches, Foreward, 1963.

Althausen, Johannes, Comp. christian Afrikas auf dem Wege Zur Freiheit. Zsgest, U. mite. Einf. vers. von Johannes Althausen. Erlangen Verl. d. eu (angelisch) -luth (erischen) mission (1971).

Beauer, Robert Pierce. *Christianity and African Education; The Papers of a Conference at the University of Chicago.* Grand Rapids, W.B. Erdmans Publishing Co., 1966.

Berman, Edward H. *African Reactions to Missionary Education.* New York: Teachers College Press, Teachers College, Columbia University, 1975.

Best, Kenneth Y. *African Challenge.* Nairobi, Kenya: Transafrica Publishers, 1975.

Callender, Timothy. *Religion: The Basis of African Culture,* Bridgetown, Barbados: Yoruba, 1977.

Coleman, James S. "Traditionalism and Nationalism in Tropical Africa," in Martin Kilson, ed., *New States in the Modern World.* Cambridge University Press, 1975.

Cragg, Kenneth. *The Privilege of Man.* London: The Athlone Press, 1968.

D'Arcy, M.C. *The Meaning and Matter of History: A Christian View.* New York: The Noonday Press, 1959.

Davidson, Basil. *The African Awakening,* London: Jonathan Cape, 1955. *Black Star: A View of the Life and Times of Kwame Nkrumah.* London: Allen Lane, 1973.

Deasi, Ram, ed. *Christianity in Africa as Seen by Africans.* Denuer, A. Swallow, 1962.

Dia, Mamadou. *The African Nations and World Solidarity.* New York: Frederick A. Praeger, 1961.

Dickson, Dwesi and Paul Ellingsworth, *Biblical Revelation and African Beliefs.* Maryknoll, New York: Orbis Books, 1969.

Dougall, James W. *Christians in the African Revolution.* Edinburgh: Saint Andrew Press, 1963.

Ellul, Jacques. *The Technological Society.* New York: Vantage Books, 1964.

Fage, J.D. *A History of Africa.* New York: Alfred A. Knopf, 1978.

Fanon, Frantz, *The Wretched of the Earth.* New York: Grover Press, Inc., 1963.

Fasholl-Luke, Edward. *Christianity in Independent Africa.* Bloomington, Indiana: Indiana University Press, 1978.

Ferkiss, Victor. *Africa's Search for Identity.* New York: George Braziller, 1966.

Groves, Charles Pelham. *Christianity in Africa.* London: Lutterworth Press, 1964.

Haselbarth, Hans. *Christian Ethics in the African Context.* Ibadan: Daystar Press, 1976.

Hassan, Yusuf Fadl. *The Arabs and the Sudan.* Khartoum, Sudan: Khartoum University Press, 1973.

Hastings, Adrian. *African Christianity.* New York: Seabury Press, 1977.

Hastings, Adrian. *African Christianity: An Essay in Interpretation.* London: G. Chapman, 1976.

Hastings, Adrian. *A History of African Christianity. 1950-75.* Cambridge/ New York: Cambridge University Press, 1979. (African Studies Series 26)

Hayward, V.E.W. ed. *African Independent Church Movements.* New York: Friendship Press, 1965.

Herskovits, Melville. *The Human Factor in Changing Africa.* New York: Vintage Books, 1962.

Ibn Khaldun, *Histoire de Berberes.* Translated de Slave, 4 Vols., Paris: 1925-46.

Idowu, E. Bolaji. *African Traditional Religion.* Maryknoll, New York: Orbis Books, 1973.

Ilogu, Edmund. *Christianity and Ibo Culture.* Leiden: E. J. Brill, 1974.

International African Seminar, 7th. University of Ghana, 1965. *Christianity in Tropical Africa; Studies Presented and Discussed at the Seventh International African Seminar,* University of Ghana, April, 1965. London, published for the International Africa Institute by Oxford University Press, 1968.

Iruine, Cecelia. *The Church of Christ in Zaire: A Handbook of*

Protestant Churches, Missions and Communities, 1878-1978. Division of Overseas Ministries, Christian Church (Disciples of Christ,) 1978.

Jahn, Janheinz. *Muntu-An Outline of African Culture.* New York: Grove Press, 1961.

July, Robert W. *The Origins of Modern African Thought.* New York: Frederick Praeger, 1967.

Kahler, Eric. *The Meaning of History.* New York: George Braziller, 1964.

King, Noel Quinton. *Christian and Muslim in Africa.* New York: Harger & Row, 1971.

Knox, *The Humanity and Divinity of Christ.* London & New York: Cambridge University Press, 1967.

Latsurette, Kenneth Scott. *A History of the Expansion of Christianity.* Grand Rapids, Michigan: Londervan Publishing House, 1970.

Leeuwen, Arend Theodor van. *Christianity in World History.* New York: Charles Scribner's Sons, 1964.

Legum, Colin. *Pan-Africanism — A Short Political Guide.* Westport, Connecticut: Greenwood Press, 1972.

Lewis, I.W. *Islam in Tropical Africa.* London: Oxford University Press, 1966.

Macdonald, Allan John. *Trade Politics and Christianity in Africa and the East,* New York: Negro Universities Press, 1969.

Macdonald, Allan John. *Christianity in Africa and the East.* New York: Negro Universities Press, 1969.

Martin, B.G. *Muslim Brotherhoods in Nineteenth Century - Africa.* Cambridge: University University Press, 1976.

Martin, Marie Louise. *Prophetic Christianity in the Congo; the Church of Christ on Earth Through the Prophet Simon Kimbanger.* Braamfontern, Christian Institute of Southern Africa, 1968.

Mazrui, Ali A. *The Political Sociology of the English Language.* The Hague and Paris: Moulton & Co., 1975.

Mazrui, Ali A. *World Culture and the Black Experience.* Seattle, Washington: University of Washington Press, 1974.

Mazrui, Ali A. *Towards a Pax Africana.* Chicago, Illinois: The University of Chicago Press, 1967.

McIntire, C.T. *God, History and Historians.* New York: Oxford University Press, 1977.

Mbiti, John S. *African Religions and Philosophy.* New York: Frederick A. Praeger, 1969.

Mbiti, John S. *Concepts of God in Africa.* New York: Frederick A. Praeger, 1970.

Mbiti, John S. *The Crisis of the Mission in Africa.* Mukono, Uganda Church Press, 1971.

Mestral, Cloude de. *Christian Literature in Africa.* International Committee on Christian Literature for Africa, 1959.

McVeigh, Malcolm J. *God in Africa; Conceptions of God in African Traditional Religion and Christianity.* Cloude Stock, Cape Cod, Massachusetts, 1954.

Missionaries to Yourselves; African Cathecists Today. Edited by Aylard Shorter and Eugene Kataza, Maryknoll, New York: Orbis, 1972.

A New Look at Christianity in Africa. Contributions by Donald R. Jacobs et al. Geneva World Student Christian Federation, 1972.

Neill, Bishop Stephen. *Twentieth Century Christianity.* Garden City, New York: Frederick A. Praeger, 1961.

Newington, David. ed. *The Shape of Personality in African Christian Leadership.* Nelspruit, South Africa. Emmanuel Press, 1962.

New Testament Christianity for Africa and the World: Essays in Honour of Harry Sawyer. London: S.P.C.K., 1974.

Nkrumah, Kwame. *I Speak of Freedom, A Statement of African Ideology.* New York: Frederick A. Praeger, 1961.

Nkrumah, K. *Neo-Colonialism.* New York: International Publishers, 1965.

Nkrumah, K. *Consciencism.* New York: Monthly Review Press, 1964.

Nkrumah, K. *Africa Must Unite.* New York: International Publishers, 1963.

Nkrumah, K. *Class Struggle in Africa.* New York: International Publishers, 1970.

Nkrumah, K. *Two Myths.* A pamphlet published by Panaf Publishers, 1970.

Northcott, William Cecil. *Christianity in Africa.* Philadelphia: Westminister Press, 1963.

Ogot, B.A. and J.A. Kieran. *Zamani: A Survey of East African History.* New York: Humanities Press, 1971.

Okwuoso, V.E. Akubueze. *In the Name of Christianity: The Missionaries in Africa.* Philadelphia, Pennsylvania: Dorrance, 1977.

Oliver, Ronald. ed. *The Dawn of African History.* London: Oxford University Press, 1969.

Oosthuizen, Gerhardus Cornelis. *Post-Christianity in Africa; A Theological and Anthropological Study.* Grand Rapids, Michigan: Eerdman's Publishing Co., 1968.

Parrinder, E.G. *African Traditional Religions.* New York: Harper and Row, 1970.

Pyle, Eric H. *Introducing Christianity.* Hammondsworth, Middlesex: Penguin Books, 1961.

Sanneh, L.O. *The Jahanke.* London: International Africa Institute, 1979.

Sawyer, Harry. *Creative Evangelism: Towards a New Christian Encounter with Africa.* London: Lutterworth Press, 1968.

Sawyer, Harry.*Christian Theology in Independent Africa.* 1961 (Aureol pamphlets, no. 3.)

Schuon, Frithjof. *Understanding Islam.* London: George Allen & Unwin, 1976.

Senghor, Leopold Sedar. *Liberte 1: Negritude et Humanisme.* Paris: Le Seuil, 1964.

Senghor, L.S. *The Foundations of "Africanite" or Negritude and "Arabite."*

Paris: Presence Africaine, 1971.

Senghor, L.S. *On Socialism.* New York: Frederick A. Praeger, 1964.

Shorter, Aylard. *Prayer in the Religious Tradition of Africa.* New York/ Nairobi: Oxford University Press, 1975.

Skurnik, W.A.E. et al. *African Political Thought: Lumumba, Nkrumah and Sekou Toure.* Denver, Colorado: University of Colorado, 1967-68.

The Holy Quran, translated by Yusuf Ali.

Trimingham, J. Spencer. *A History of Islam in West Africa.* London/Oxford: Oxford University Press, 1965.

Trimingham, J.S. *Islam in West Africa.* London: Oxford University Press, 1959.

Trimingham, J.S. *The Influence of Islam Upon Africa.* London/New York 1968.

Trimingham, J.S. *Islam in Ethiopia.* London: OUP., 1952.

Turner, H.W. *African Independent Church.* 2 vols. London and New York: Oxford University Press, 1967.

Wauthier, Claude. *The Literature and Thought of Modern Africa.* Praeger Publishers, 1967.

Willis, John Ralph ed. *Studies in West African Islamic History.* London/Totowa: Frank Cass & Co., Ltd., 1979.

ARTICLES

Abdul, Musa O.A., and others, "Unity of God and the Community of Mankind: Cooperation Between African Muslims and African Christians in Work and Witness (List of Members) *Study Encounter,* vol. 11, no. 1, pp. 1-5, 1975.

Anyanwu, K.C., "African Religion as an Experienced Reality," *Thought and Practice.,* vol. 2, no. 2, 1975.

Awolalu, J. Omosade, "Sin and Its Removal in African Traditional Religion," *Journal of the American Academy of Religion,* vol. 44, pp.

275-287, June, 1976.

Ba, Amadou Hampate, "African Art, Where the Hands have Ears," *The UNESCO Courier*, February, 1971.

Brown, K.I., "Color and Christian Missions in Africa," *Journal of Religious Thought*. vol. 23, no. 1., pp. 51-59, 1966-67.

Carr, Burgess. The Crisis of the African Christian Press. s. AFR. OUTLOOK, (Capte Town), 103, 1228, Sept. 1973: 146-7, 157.

"Engagement of Lusake, Zambia (All Africa Conference of Churches, 3d, 1974) *IDOC* Bulletin No. 22, pp. 2-10, August, 1974.

"Internationalizing the Mission" *IDOC/International Documentation*, No. 63, pp 72-4, July, 1974.

"Lusakas Uppfordran;" translated by B.G.M. Sundkler, *Svensk Missionstidskrift*, vol. 62, no. 3, pp. 115-27, 1974.

"Christianity in Post-Colonial Africa" *IDOC Bulletin* no. 18, p. 14, April, 1974.

Christian Press in Africa: Voice of Human Concern. Lusaka, Zambia: Multimedia Publications, 1973.

Crawford, John Ruhard. *Protestant Missions in Congo, 1878-1969. (n.p.)* 1969.

Dammann, Ernst. *Das Christentum in Afrika.* Munchen, Hamburg, Siehenstern-Taschenbueh-Verlag, (1968).

De Mestral, Claude. *Christian Literature in Africa.* London, distributed by the Christian Literature Council, 1959.

Fashole-Luke, Edward W., "Quest for African Christian Theologies," *Scottish Journal of Theology*, vol. 29, no. 2, pp. 159-175, 1976.

Imasogie, O., "African Traditional Religion and Christian Faith," *Review and Expositor*, vol. 70, pp. 283-93, summer, 1973.

Jah, Omar, "Islamic History in West Sudan," *Journal of the Muslim World League*, (Jan., 1978).

Kalanda, Paul, "Consolidating Christianity in Africa," *Missiology*

Vol. 4, pp. 395-404, October, 1976.

Kastfelt, Niels, "African Prophetism and Christian Missionaries in Northeast Nigeria," *Journal of Religion in Africa,* vol. 8, no. 3, pp. 175-188, 1976.

Kato, Byang H., "Christian Surge in Africa," Part 1; Africa's Christian Future, Part 2 (Interview) *Christianity Today,* vol. 19, 4-7 September 26, 12-16 October 10, 1975.

Kafi, Kuba, "Church's Healing Ministry in Africa" (bibliography) *The Ecumenical Review,* vol. 27, pp. 230-239, July, 1975.

Makunike, E.C., "Evangelism in the Cultural Context of Africa," *International Review of Missions,* vol. 63, pp. 57-63, January, 1974.

Mugambi, J.N.K., "The African Experience of God," *Thought and Practice,* Vol. 1, no. 1, 1974.

Mbiti, John S., "African Views American Black Theology," *World View,* vol. 17, pp. 41-4, August, 1974.

Murray, Jocelyn and Walls, A.F., "Study of Religion in East, Central and Southern Africa," *Religion,* vol. 5, pp. 94-98, Special Issue, August, 1975.

Nyang, Sulayman S., "The Islamic State and Economic Development: A Theoretical Analysis," *Islamic Culture,* Vol. 50, no. 1, 1976.

Nyang, Sulayman S., "Islam and Pan-Africanism," *L'Afrique et L'Asie Modemes,* no. 104 (1975).

"Wholeness of Human Life; Christian Involvement in Mankind's Inner Dialogue with Primal World-Views (Exploratory Consultation," Institute of Church and Society, Ibadan, Nigeria, 1973; bibliography) *Study Encounter,* vol. 9, no. 4, pp. 1-20 SE '52 '73.